PENGUIN BOOKS
MODERN CONSERVATISM

David Willetts was educated at King Edward's School, Birmingham, and at Oxford where he took a first in Philosophy, Politics and Economics. He served as an official in HM Treasury from 1978 to 1984, including a spell as Private Secretary to Nigel Lawson. He was then a member of Mrs Thatcher's Downing Street Policy Unit. Since 1987 he has been Director of Studies at the Centre for Policy Studies. He is also Consultant Director of the Conservative Research Department. He has been closely involved in the development of Conservative policy over the past decade, and has written widely on economic and social issues. He is Prospective Conservative Parliamentary Candidate for Havant in Hampshire.

D1338399

To Sarah

DAVID WILLETTS

MODERN CONSERVATISM

PENGUIN BOOKS

PENGUIN BOOKS

Published by the Penguin Group
Penguin Books Ltd, 27 Wrights Lane, London W8 5TZ, England
Penguin Books USA Inc., 375 Hudson Street, New York, New York 10014, USA
Penguin Books Australia Ltd, Ringwood, Victoria, Australia
Penguin Books Canada Ltd, 10 Alcorn Avenue, Toronto, Ontario, Canada M4V 3B2
Penguin Books (NZ) Ltd, 182–190 Wairau Road, Auckland 10, New Zealand

Penguin Books Ltd, Registered Offices: Harmondsworth, Middlesex, England
First published 1992
1 3 5 7 9 10 8 6 4 2

Printed in England by Clays Ltd, St Ives plc
Set in 10/12 pt Times

CONTENTS

INTRODUCTION

Our house in Havant lies between two Victorian pubs. One is the Richard Cobden, named after the great nineteenth-century campaigner for free trade. The other is rather more traditional – the Prince of Wales. I do not know if any ancient political enmities divided them. But the purpose of this book is to show why a Conservative can happily drink in both establishments.

The book is not intended to suggest new Conservative policies for the next decade, nor does it review exciting developments in conservatism in other countries. Its purpose is much more modest: to be a straightforward guide to British conservatism – its history, its principles, its policies.

This book could only be written because of many a stimulating conversation with friends on the subject over the years. There is only space to acknowledge my greatest debts here. I had the great good fortune as an undergraduate to be tutored in political philosophy by Dr John Gray. He is a teacher who has become a friend. I am grateful to him for many illuminating discussions of the issues in this book. I am also grateful to Samuel Brittan, Nigel Lawson, and former colleagues from my days as a Treasury official, for introducing me to the world of economic policy. I had the privilege of working for Mrs Thatcher for three years in her Downing Street Policy Unit, and then serving as Director of Studies at the Centre for Policy Studies – the think-tank which she helped to found. She will always be one of my political heroes. The board of directors of the Centre for Policy Studies have been enlightened and tolerant employers; I am grateful to them for the opportunity to participate in the debate about the direction of conservatism over the past five years.

Samuel Brittan, John Butterfield, Peter Cropper, Clive Froggatt, John Gray, Gervas Huxley, Robert O'Brien and Anthony Teasdale all kindly commented on an earlier draft of this book. John Hanvey of the Harris Research Centre generously assisted with the polling figures. My editor at Penguin, Jon Riley, has been a model of benign wisdom, as has my copy editor, Patricia Taylor Chalmers. The remaining errors of fact and judgement are my responsibility alone.

It is not enough to thank Frances Hawkins for typing – and retyping – the book. She has also been an indefatigable sub-editor and a most enterprising researcher. I am most grateful to her for all her work over the past year.

Finally, I thank my wife Sarah – to whom this book is dedicated. Without her it would not exist.

DAVID WILLETTS

PART I:

HISTORY

CHAPTER I:

The Tory Tradition

Conservatives are wary of grand statements of principles and beliefs. Many attribute the political success of British conservatism to its pragmatism – its concern with political practice not political theory. Anything which goes further than this is dismissed as ideology – and that is for socialists or libertarians. There is an opposing view which argues that Conservatives do indeed have a distinctive view of the world which does yield political principles. Moreover any party which is perpetually chopping and changing to keep up with the vagaries of popular opinion will lose its self-respect and the respect of the electorate. T. S. Eliot showed how to resolve this argument in his essay on 'The Literature of Politics':

> ... political thinking, that is, thinking that concerns itself with the permanent principles, if any, underlying a party name, can follow two contrasted lines of development. At the beginning may be a body of doctrine, perhaps a canonical work; and a band of devoted people set out to disseminate and popularize this doctrine through its emotional appeal to the interested and the disinterested; and then, as a political party, endeavour to realize a programme based on the doctrine. Before arriving at the position of governing, they have envisaged some final state of society of which their doctrines give the outline. The theory has altogether preceded the practice.
>
> But political ideas may come into being by an opposite process. A political party may find that it has had a history, before it is fully aware of or agreed upon its own permanent tenets; it may have arrived at its actual formation through a succession of metamorphoses and adaptations, during which some issues have been superannuated and new issues have arisen. What its fundamental tenets are, will probably be found only by careful examination of its behaviour throughout its history and by examination

of what its more thoughtful and philosophic minds have said on its behalf; and only accurate historical knowledge and judicious analysis will be able to discriminate between the permanent and the transitory; between those doctrines and principles which it must ever, and in all circumstances, maintain, or manifest itself a fraud, and those called forth by special circumstances, which are only intelligible and justifiable in the light of those circumstances.[1]

The second approach – which Eliot calls the 'organic' rather than the 'mechanical' – is the best way of understanding Conservative political ideas. Conservatives do indeed have political principles – but they have emerged from political practice.

Conservatives like their ideas made flesh in particular historical figures and circumstances. It is why Conservative arguments are much more likely to turn on interpretations of history, either as name-dropping – 'a true follower of Disraeli's One Nation Toryism' – or name-calling – 'nothing but a Gladstonian Liberal'.

The case of 'Thatcherism' is the latest example of a debate about ideas being conducted around a particular person. It was attacked as somehow a break with the Conservative tradition. The Conservative party under Mrs Thatcher was supposed to have departed from traditional Toryism and been captured by a clique of free-marketeers. Thatcherism was supposed to owe more to nineteenth-century economic liberalism and the theories of continental philosophers such as Hayek, or American economists such as Friedman, than to Disraeli and Salisbury, Churchill and Macmillan. Ironically, this argument takes exactly the same form as the criticism levelled by Thatcherites against Edward Heath's administration – that abandoning sound financial policies and introducing pay and price controls took the Conservative party too far from its true self. This is how Conservatives should argue with each other – about the interpretation of their own tradition. It is essential if the Tory party is to carry on being true to itself, that it should permanently engage in a debate about its own history. Otherwise, it will indeed be unable to answer what Disraeli in *Coningsby* called 'the awkward question' of 'what will you conserve?'

What follows, in the rest of Part I of this book, is not a full history of the Conservative party. Rather, it is an attempt to highlight a few key features of Conservative history which may have been lost from sight. In particular, it aims to show that free markets and sound money are at the heart of the Conservative tradition.

The Country Party

The name 'Conservative' was first applied to a political grouping during the Reform Bill crisis of 1830–32. That grouping can be traced further back through the premiership of Liverpool (1812–27) as far as Pitt the Younger, who served as Prime Minister for much of the period from 1783 to his death in 1806. We could, more ambitiously, trace the origins of the Conservative party back to the old Tories, who opposed the Whig Settlement of 1688. This old Tory party ceases to be a distinct political group after the accession of George III as the Hanoverians came to be accepted.[2] By the mid-eighteenth century we can think of a political divide between Court and Country. These are not so much party labels but they do capture differences in attitudes and social backgrounds. The Country party comprised the local squires who were the permanent backbenchers looking with a beady eye on the conduct of government. Successful political leaders, such as Walpole and Pitt the Younger, earned their longevity in office by their ability to manage such men.

The gentlemen farmers and landowners were rather self-consciously outsiders in the London political scene. They were wary of the aristocratic Whigs, who were too metropolitan and too cosmopolitan for their taste. The Tory squires were unlikely to own an expensive London town house, but might rent one for the season; nor would they necessarily send their children on the Grand Tour. But this did not make them naïve country bumpkins. They sat as local justices of the peace and administered the local Poor Law; they knew how men were to be governed. Indeed, they probably saw this more clearly than the Whig grandees, insulated by enormous rent-rolls and tiers of servants.

They were wary of foreign entanglements because that meant

bigger government and higher taxation. They did not trust the City financiers who lent the government the money to finance the wars, because they knew it was their taxes which then serviced the debt (David Ricardo's economics showed that government borrowing was just taxation deferred). In short, they were opposed to what Disraeli described in his novel *Sybil* as 'Venetian politics, Dutch finance and French wars' – rule by an aristocratic élite, public borrowing and foreign adventures.

Nowadays conservatism is denounced by its critics as just the ethos of the small town businessman or shopkeeper. Conservatives reply by attacking the silliness of the chattering classes who never have to run anything. There is nothing new about this. It is indeed Country versus Whig. It is practical (if blinkered) wisdom versus wrong-headed (if sophisticated) cleverness. One thinks of Lady Antonia Fraser's socialist salon meeting in Holland Park within a few hundred yards of the remains of the house where Lord Holland hosted grand Whig parties two hundred years ago. His sympathy with the French Revolution shocked the mass of the population then. The Conservatives have never been the party of the *bien pensants*.

This may sound like depressing confirmation that the Conservative party is the 'stupid party'.[3] But that is to misunderstand the point. Some of the very greatest thinkers and writers have been conservative – from David Hume to T. S. Eliot. The point is that conservatism respects, and is indeed rooted in, the unreflective, but deeply felt, values of the normal citizen. It is the opposite of left-wing radicalism with its arrogant idea of false consciousness: that most of the electorate do not truly understand the political and economic events swirling around them, whereas an élite have been given an insight into the real nature of society and their task is to shake the masses from their slumbers.

The Conservative, by contrast, respects the practical man. In Britain at its best, that common sense is so deep and powerful as to become true wisdom. The Conservative party has long been the party of the silent majority. As Burke put it:

Because half a dozen grasshoppers under a fern make the field ring with their importunate chink, whilst thousands of great cattle, reposed beneath the shadow of the British oak, chew the cud and are silent, pray do not imagine, that those who make the noise are the only inhabitants of the field; that of course, they are many in number; or that, after all, they are other than the little, shrivelled, meagre, hopping, though loud and troublesome *insects* of the hour.[4]

The End of Mercantilism

There is a conventional picture of British history as the steady, and apparently inexorable, spread of state involvement in the economy and society, at least until the election of an 'extremist' Conservative government in 1979 uniquely committed to reversing this trend. For Conservatives this helped give Mrs Thatcher's government its heroic quality, and for socialists made it specially outrageous.

This is bad history. One could identify a series of turning points in British history when men of property, representing our tradition of individualism, have resisted the encroachment of the state. The period from the end of the Napoleonic wars in 1815 to the repeal of the Corn Laws in 1846 is dominated by another bold project to roll back the frontiers of the state. Some of the major figures in the early history of conservatism were crucially involved.

Adam Smith's argument for free markets in his *Wealth of Nations* (published in 1776) was not a defence of the status quo, but an attack on it. It was not a summary of the conventional economic wisdom of the time, but a brilliant critique of the dominant economic doctrine of seventeenth- and eighteenth-century Britain – mercantilism – which encouraged detailed state intervention in the economy with the object of building up the nation's stock of bullion. The Navigation Acts banned foreign ships from carrying British cargoes; only the East India Company was allowed to trade beyond the Cape of Good Hope; the 1662 Settlement Laws severely restricted migration of labour within the country; the Corn Laws banned grain imports unless the domestic price was above eighty shillings a quarter; usury laws limited interest to a maximum of five per cent; and the state still had the power to regulate wages. (Many of these regulations were more honoured in the breach than the observance. There was a large black economy. Indeed, what better way to keep men of commerce in their place than to drive them perilously close to illegality?) The old aristocratic establishment were happy to preside over such arrangements; after all, they created scope for them to use their powers of patronage and place relatives and supporters in lucrative posts administering this ramshackle state apparatus. And if the state did not raise revenue by these indirect taxes, it might be driven to tax their incomes direct.

Adam Smith led the intellectual assault on the mercantilist conventional wisdom. Edmund Burke was a powerful advocate of Adam Smith's political economy. Indeed, Smith believed that Burke had anyway reached these views independently and said of him: 'that he was the only man who, without communication, thought on these topics exactly as he did'. Burke's views are set out most starkly in his *Thoughts and Details on Scarcity*, which was originally a private memorandum to Pitt arguing against regulation of the grain supply. The intellectual atmosphere then was pithily described by Walter Bagehot a hundred years later. He said that the doctrine of free trade was indeed 'in the air', but it was not accepted or established; 'on the contrary, it was a tenet against which a respectable parent would probably caution his son; – still it was known as a tempting heresy against which a warning was needed'.[5]

Pitt the Younger was probably the first leading politician to absorb these ideas. The Eden Treaty of 1786, lowering tariffs between Britain and France, is the earliest example of the influence of Smith's ideas in practice. But the Napoleonic wars put back the cause of economic reform from the 1780s to the 1820s. It was Lord Liverpool's magnificent, underrated 'liberal Tory' administration of 1812–27 which really began the process of deregulation that culminated in the premiership of Peel. Sadly, his government is now remembered above all for the 'Peterloo massacre' of 1819 when about a dozen radical demonstrators died. But overall its handling of political and social tensions after the Napoleonic wars compares well with our experience after the First and Second World Wars.

The first task was to put the public finances on a sound basis, after the Napoleonic wars (80 per cent of revenues were going to service the National Debt). The budget was brought into surplus and the 1819 currency legislation led to a rapid return to the gold standard. This sound financial policy was matched by the first moves to end the old mercantilist system. Norman Gash conveys the significance of the shift:

> Liverpool's great free-trade speech of 26 May 1820 was the first time that a British prime minister firmly and unequivocally stated the advantages of an unrestricted freedom of trade. Some contended, he observed, that Britain had risen to greatness because of her protective system. 'Others, of whom I am one, believe that we have risen in spite of that system.'[6]

The first liberalizing legislation was passed in 1821, five Acts followed in 1822, and the momentum continued through the rest of the 1820s. Monopolies were restricted, the Navigation Act relaxed, customs duties reduced and simplified, and restrictions on exports were largely abandoned.

The Whig governments of the 1830s saw little further progress on free trade, but Liverpool's protégés finished the job under Peel's administration of 1841–6. The budget of 1842 repealed the duty on 750 items. Finally, and most famously, the Corn Laws were repealed in 1846: agriculture was no longer to be protected from cheap foreign imports. But it was not just a matter of getting government out of detailed economic regulation. At the same time, the reformers set in place a new financial structure which gave the government the necessary control over monetary policy. The Bank Charter Act of 1844 made the power of issuing currency the exclusive prerogative of the Bank of England, and the Bank took its current form, divided into the Banking Department and the Issue Department, so that it could not simply print more money to finance government debt. This mixture of deregulation and sound money is now called 'monetarism' (see Chapter IX).

The success of this strategy of withdrawing the state from many areas of economic activity was the basis of mid-Victorian prosperity and confidence. It required courage as well as political skill to take on vested interests. Victorian prosperity did not just appear; it was the result of an explicit programme of deregulation, liberalization and tax-cutting carried out by leading politicians over several decades going back to an intellectual assault on the conventional wisdom led by Adam Smith and Edmund Burke. It all begins to sound rather familiar! It was a predominantly conservative achievement. But the Conservative party was split by the repeal of the Corn Laws and so went out of office for a generation – enabling the Liberals to preside over the prosperity engendered by economic reform.

This economic reform programme had an impact on the political culture. The shift from the corruption and patronage systems of eighteenth-century politics to the high moral tone of Victorian politics was partly the result of the state's economic disengagement. The scope for politicians to give special favours to lobbyists and interest groups was limited. Winston Churchill put his finger on this when he opposed the reintroduction of tariffs in the 1900s because it would lead to 'the Americanization of British politics'; it would have brought back the jobbing and the selling of political favours which came with government intervention in trade through tariffs.

This fascinating historical episode – the free-market reforms of early nineteenth-century England – shows not just the longstanding links between conservatism and free markets, but also that such economic policies do in the long term elevate, not debase, a nation's political culture.

Disraeli and One Nation Conservatism

Disraeli opposed what he saw as a commercial, utilitarian element in conservatism. Lord Liverpool was dismissed as the 'Arch-Mediocrity'. Peel, one of the great Conservative reformers, got even rougher treatment because he stood in the way of Disraeli's promotion. By turning his brilliant sardonic pen to attacking the leading Conservatives of the first half of the nineteenth century, Disraeli did a profound and long-lasting disservice to the Conservative party's understanding of its own history. Instead of taking pride in the greatest programme of free-market economic reforms the country was to see for over a century, Disraeli led Conservatives to associate this, guiltily, with boot-faced mill-owners.

Disraeli was right to see that conservatism is not mechanistic, Benthamite utilitarianism. That particular view of the world was only held by the purist nineteenth-century liberals: it is much too bleak and materialistic for a Conservative. There was a distinctive contribution that conservatism could make to the anxious discussion of the 'condition of England' question in the 1840s. The extraordinary passage in his novel *Sybil* describing the two nations, can still send a *frisson* of emotion through any thoughtful Conservative:

'Two nations; between whom there is no intercourse and no sympathy; who are as ignorant of each other's habits, thoughts, and feelings, as if they were dwellers in different zones, or inhabitants of different planets; who are formed by a different breeding, are fed by a different food, are ordered by different manners, and are not governed by the same laws.'

'You speak of –' said Egremont, hesitatingly.

'THE RICH AND THE POOR.'[7]

Disraeli understood that Conservatives must have some vision of community that the rationalist, economic utilitarians could not grasp. He was right to identify 'One Nation' as a powerful theme in conservative thought, which it remains to this day. But he had no real idea of where to take this insight, nor how to fit it into the experience of nineteenth-century England as it industrialized. Hence he retreated into nostalgia for the Middle Ages. That famous passage quoted above occurs immediately after a long section in praise of the medieval monasteries. As a result, his contribution to the development of Conservative political ideas is no greater than the contribution of the medievalist Pre-Raphaelites to the development of British art. He failed to understand what Burke had appreciated: that a successful, coherent conservatism has to tie together free-market economics and a sense of community. Had Disraeli grasped this, he would not have seen his commitment to social reform as the opposite of the economic reforms of Liverpool and Peel. He would have recognized that repealing the old customs duties, or getting rid of the Corn Laws to lower the price of workers' bread, were in themselves great social reforms. They were a contribution to improving the condition of England too. They could stand beside the abolition of slavery, achieved by the Tory Wilberforce, and the Factory Acts ensuring basic working conditions for which the Tory Shaftesbury campaigned so vigorously.

Ironically, whatever Disraeli's rhetoric, his actual policy measures as Prime Minister in 1867–8, and then 1874–80, were much closer to the mid-Victorian free-market consensus. As sometimes happens in the British parliamentary system, his great debating duels with Gladstone disguised the extent to which they agreed on fundamentals. Disraeli stuck as resolutely as Gladstone to three great economic principles: the value of the pound was fixed by the gold standard; the government's budget was small and, usually, in surplus; and trade was unregulated. Indeed, the spirit of free trade was so powerful that one Victorian cabinet debated whether it was right to restrict the import of beef known to be infected with foot and mouth disease. Adam Smith's free-market project had so comprehensively triumphed that it was not any longer a matter of political dispute. It provided the ground rules of High Victorian politics. Gladstone and Disraeli did not argue about that. When critics of Mrs Thatcher denounced her as a Gladstonian liberal with no understanding of Disraeli's conservatism, they overlooked the crucial point: in the area of economics, modern conservatism adheres to the ideas which Disraeli and Gladstone held in common.

Disraeli did add one distinctive element to conservatism, however; he largely invented the idea of the British Empire (though Britain had long had overseas possessions). But whatever the rhetoric, this imperial idea was in practice always subordinated to Disraeli's commitment to free trade and the free market. He did not make the mistake of trying to make the Empire a protectionist economic bloc – the temptation to which the Conservative party succumbed fifty years later. The abolition of the sugar duties in the first budget of his new government in 1874 effectively destroyed the economies of the British West Indies, which lost out to cheaper producers such as Cuba. Cheap sugar for British workers was more important than the Empire.

If anything, he saw the British Empire as part of his populist cause of winning over the craftsmen and artisans enfranchised by his Reform Act of 1867. Indeed, one of his great electoral achievements for the Conservative party was to discern what his *Times* obituary called 'the angels in marble' – the skilled, working-class Tories, the group that psephologists now call the C2s. Disraeli would have admired the performance of the Conservative party a century after his death in reaching out to the skilled working class, winning 40 per cent of its vote, more than the Labour party, in the general elections of 1983 and 1987 (40 per cent Conservative, 32 per cent Labour in 1983; 40 per cent Conservative, 36 per cent Labour in 1987: MORI).

There is one feature of British imperialism which marks it out from some other great empires, and gives it an unusual quality. Whilst some other empires make bloated claims to be permanent, Conservatives always recognized that the British Empire would not last. After all, the loss of the American colonies and the virtual autonomy given to Canada after the Durham reforms, had shown that one could not hold on to overseas possessions for ever. That it was an empire on which the sun never set was a fact about its geography, not a claim about its permanence. Because they understand history, Conservatives also understand transience. It is one reason for the conservative tendency to melancholy, to which I now turn.

The Marquess of Salisbury and Herbert Spencer

Robert Cecil, third Marquess of Salisbury, Conservative Prime Minister in 1885–6, 1886–92, and 1895–1902, represents a distinctive quality in conservatism: a sense of how fleeting is human achievement – in politics, if not in art and literature – and anxiety that things are getting worse. This cast of mind can easily become a caricature of itself, descending into muddle-headed nostalgia and affected fogeyism. But he transcended these emotions to give distinctively conservative insights into his age and the rise of socialism.[8] Herbert Spencer, an almost exact contemporary, is in many ways a striking contrast to Salisbury. He was no Conservative. He was an extreme individualist and denounced exactly the sort of tradition of hierarchical Toryism which Disraeli embraced. But this unlikely duo of bearded late-Victorian sages both saw, very early on, a shift in thinking about the rôle of the state. By the 1880s Spencer was denouncing the modest reformist legislation of late-Victorian governments as a fundamental attack on our personal freedoms and on the principles of free trade. Dickens had already caricatured the hysterical attitude of some free-marketeers and commercial interests towards any government regulation in *Hard Times*:

> They were ruined, when they were required to send labouring children to school; they were ruined, when inspectors were appointed to look into their works; they were ruined when such inspectors considered it doubtful whether they were quite justified in chopping people up with their machinery; they were utterly undone, when it was hinted that perhaps they need not always make quite so much smoke.[9]

Spencer exposed himself to that sort of criticism because of the great passion with which he denounced the government regulations of the Victorian period. He wrote of what he called 'the coming slavery'. Reading him today, one is overwhelmed by the power and coherence of his arguments yet taken aback by the targets at which they are aimed. They are a brilliant demolition of the idea of government planning. But did he really need to turn all this vehemence on the Bakehouses Regulation Act of 1863?

Spencer has an answer to this line of criticism. It is that the 'practical' politician:

goes on thinking only of proximate results, naturally never thinks of results still more remote, still more general . . . he never asks whether the political momentum set up by his measure . . . may not . . . presently [produce] an aggregate energy working changes never thought of. Dwelling only on the effects of his particular stream of legislation, and not observing how such other streams already existing, and still other streams which will follow his initiative, pursue the same average course, it never occurs to him that they may presently unite into a voluminous flood utterly changing the face of things.[10]

Spencer is significant because he understood the trend of political ideas. In particular he saw the deep change that took place in the Liberal party in the 1880s. Whereas it had been the pre-eminent custodian of free trade, it began to succumb to the 'New Liberalism' of economic and social regulation:

The laws made by Liberals are so greatly increasing the compulsions and restraints exercised over citizens, that among conservatives who suffer from this aggressiveness there is growing opportunity to resist it. Proof is furnished by the fact that the 'Liberty and Property Defence League', largely consisting of conservatives, has taken for its motto 'Individualism *versus* Socialism'. So that if the present drift of things continues, it may by and by really happen that the Tories will be defenders of liberties which the Liberals, in pursuit of what they think popular welfare, trample under foot.[11]

Spencer not only understood that he was living through the resurgence of faith in the power of government regulation, he also saw that – whatever the rhetoric of Disraeli – the Conservative party would become the party of freedom opposing these changes.

Salisbury reached similar conclusions from a different line of thought. Only a few months before Spencer wrote his essay on the New Toryism, Salisbury produced his famous article of 1883 in the *Quarterly Review*, simply entitled 'Disintegration'. He wrote that:

Freedom greatly tends to the increase of industry and commerce; and as they increase, wealth is accumulated, and inequalities of fortune necessarily become more and more marked. For some not very evident reason, they are borne more impatiently than the inequalities of an aristocratic type, which have almost always originated in conquest. After some time the contest becomes very intense. Vast multitudes have not had the chance of accumulating or have neglected it, and whenever the stream of prosperity slackens for a time, privation overtakes the large crowds who have no reserve, and produces widespread suffering ... The organiser of decay, the Radical agitator, soon makes his appearance under these conditions. He easily persuades those who are too wretched, and have thought too carelessly to see through his sophistry, that political arrangements are the causes of differences of wealth, and that by trusting him with political power they will be redressed. He does not tell his dupes how it is possible they should live if industry languishes, or how industry and enterprise can flourish if men conceive the fear, that the harvest of wealth which they and theirs have sown and reaped and stored may perchance be wrested from them by the politicians. Then arises that long conflict between possession and non-possession which was the fatal disease of free communities in ancient times, and which threatens so many nations of the present.[12]

This anxiety about the nature of modern politics explains Salisbury's extraordinarily pessimistic remarks. Thus he wrote in 1882, for example: 'It will be interesting to be the last of the conservatives. I foresee that will be our fate.'[13] But pessimism is not the same as fatalism and Salisbury proved to be a great Conservative leader because he acted to try and steer these changes in a Conservative direction. Disraeli might have been the first to spot the 'new angels in marble' but Salisbury was the first Conservative to get out and address them at mass meetings – no fewer than seventy outside Westminster between 1881 and 1885. He took much more interest than Disraeli had done in the organization of the Conservative party in the big industrial cities. He backed the Liberal government's extension of the franchise in 1884 because he saw the electoral potential of the new 'villa

Toryism'. He was trying to create a new Toryism that linked the landed and industrial interests in a defence of freedom against the encroachment of the state.

Salisbury steered through the realignment of British politics which Spencer had described. Having been, under Disraeli, the party whose rhetoric was about moderating free-market economic liberalism, the party was now the defender of liberty against the increasingly interventionist Liberals and the rise of socialism. In a speech in 1882 he declared: 'In respect to personal freedom the issues of politics are shifting. The Liberal party is less every day the party that supports liberty.'[14] Spencer and Salisbury had understood very early on what was to be the pattern of British politics throughout most of the twentieth century.

Underlying these particular insights, at a particular point in British history, there is a more general conservative disposition. This is an ambivalence about progress, and an awareness of the costs of change. Conservatives have not aimed, like some reactionary continental movements, to halt all change. Indeed, it is because the conservative recognizes that change is both inevitable and costly that there is often a note of melancholy in British conservative thought, as is conveyed in the following beautiful passage from Oakeshott:

> A storm which sweeps away a copse and transforms a favourite view, the death of friends, the sleep of friendship, the desuetude of customs of behaviour, the retirement of a favourite clown, involuntary exile, reversals of fortune, the loss of abilities enjoyed and their replacement by others – these are changes, none perhaps without its compensations, which the man of conservative temperament unavoidably regrets.[15]

It is this sense of loss which makes some art distinctively conservative – one thinks of the music of Elgar, the poetry of Philip Larkin. This may seem out of tune with the buoyant, confident conservatism of the 1980s and 1990s. But Salisbury's appreciation of the forces driving social and political change did not lead to total passivity. He acted to try to ensure change was consistent with conservative principles.

CHAPTER II:

The Advance of Socialism: 1900–1950

British politics in the first half of the twentieth century is dominated by one transcendently great leader – Winston Churchill. He appears early on as a bold, Liberal reformer, second only to Lloyd George in energy and vision. In the 1920s he is the Conservative Chancellor who must bear some responsibility for the Great Depression by running what we would now call an excessively tight monetary policy. After his years in the wilderness, he emerges as the great war leader who also encouraged junior ministers in his Coalition government to develop their ideas for extending the welfare state. But his extraordinary career cannot disguise the fact that it was during this period that conservatism suffered its greatest reverses. The fears of Lord Salisbury and Herbert Spencer about the rise of socialist collectivism proved all too true.

Some historians see the first half of the twentieth century as a period of Conservative electoral domination, and debate 'the strange death of Liberal England'. But equally the period can be seen as encompassing the strange decline of Conservative England. Conservatives rarely seemed to have the initiative. The period begins with the Liberal landslide of 1906 and ends with the Labour landslide of 1945. In between there were remarkably few occasions when Conservatives governed on their own – with a Conservative prime minister and a Conservative majority in the House of Commons (the Bonar Law and Baldwin governments of 1922–3 and Baldwin's government of 1924–9, though one might also include the 'National' governments of Baldwin and Chamberlain, 1935–40). Admittedly Conservatives were in office for much longer, but in governments led by others: under Asquith and Lloyd George 1915–22, and MacDonald 1931–5; or in coalition with others such as the War Cabinet of 1940–45. These long periods serving in government with others show conservatism on the defensive. The political initiative lay first with the Liberals and then with the Labour party. It is a classic example of the political damage caused by losing the battle of ideas.

There were three types of assault on the Conservative position which will be looked at in turn. First there was the erosion of Victorian conventions encouraged by the Bloomsbury Group. It is the first and most conspicuous example of that twentieth-century phenomenon, the bourgeois counter-culture. Then there was the emergence of an alternative socialist programme, developed above all by Fabians. Their assumptions of the rationality of the public sector and the benign effectiveness of government still have an influence. Third, and most significant of all, was the change in the industrial structure and the rise of organized labour which provided the political base for socialism. These three distinct assaults on the Conservative position remain relevant to the political debate today.

Bloomsbury

British public policy in the Victorian era rested on a set of rules and conventions which were not subject to party political dispute (as was shown in the discussion of Gladstone and Disraeli in the previous chapter). These conventions, which can be traced back to Adam Smith's revolution in economic thinking, cracked and buckled under enormous political pressures during the first half of this century.

Victorian governments had limited sources of revenue and thus limited scope for expenditure. Indeed, the abolition of mercantilist tariffs had left the state with fewer sources of revenue than it had enjoyed in the eighteenth century. High Victorian Liberals such as Gladstone had used the argument now associated with Ronald Reagan – that the inability to levy these taxes would itself act as a discipline on the legislature's extravagance. But by the end of the nineteenth century there was a growing fear of a fundamental revenue crisis affecting government as the narrowness of the tax base increasingly constrained them from embarking on projects they wanted: more finance for education, state pensions, imperial commitments. Harcourt's death duties of 1894 opened up new sources of revenue at the cost of the decline of the old landed estates. The crucial breakthrough was Lloyd George's new taxes on property in his budgets of 1909 and 1910. After the opposition of the Peers was overcome, their power to obstruct further taxes was stripped from them by the Parliament Act of 1911. One chamber of Parliament now had complete power of revenue raising. The rights of property seemed to be prey to transient majorities in one chamber. One historian regards it as the end of the 1688 Settlement 'which seemed to have made property and income, apart from taxation levels of an accepted and modest kind, inviolate against the State'.[1]

A second crucial rule – and this time it was explicit – was the gold standard. That baffling tautology on a five-pound note – the Bank of England promises 'to pay the bearer on demand the sum of five pounds' – used to mean something. It meant that you could turn up at the Bank of England and exchange a five-pound note for a fixed amount of gold. The gold standard was suspended during World War One as it had been during the Napoleonic wars. But Churchill, as Chancellor, took the fateful decision in 1925 to return to the gold standard at such a high value for the pound that it drove the economy into depression and was unsustainable. Despite the efforts by MacDonald's Labour government of 1929–31 to stay on the gold standard, it was suspended by the new National government in September 1931. Thus within twenty-five years, the entire framework of classical British political economy had been abandoned: there was little constraint on either fiscal activism or monetary laxity.

Sidney Webb, a member of the outgoing Labour government, is reputed to have said when the pound was taken off the gold standard: 'They never told us we could do that.'[2] This touching remark conveys the sense of innocence lost and applies far beyond the ambit of economic policy. It epitomizes a wider change in attitudes during the period as the *haute bourgeoisie* began to throw into doubt those tenets which the Victorians had lived by. If the Great Depression eroded respect for old economic rules, the Great War seemed to show that the old certainties and deference led to misery and carnage.

It was the Bloomsbury Group above all which tried to demolish Victorian ideas, to 'debunk' them – a word which enters the language in the 1920s. Lytton Strachey mocked the eminent Victorians with an enticing mixture of tartness and affection. Clive Bell challenged the established canon of aesthetic taste. Keynes summarized the Bloomsbury spirit:

> We repudiated entirely customary morals, conventions and traditional wisdom. We were, that is to say, in the strict sense of the term, immoralists. The consequences of being found out had, of course, to be considered for what they were worth. But we recognised no moral obligation on us, no inner sanction, to conform or to obey. Before heaven we came to be our own judge in our own case.[3]

The Bloomsbury Group exemplifies what Lionel Trilling identifies as the 'adversary culture' of the modern intellectual. As Irving Kristol observes:

> the culture that educates us – the patterns of perception and thought our children absorb in their schools, at every level – is unfriendly (at the least) to the commercial civilisation, the bourgeois civilisation, within which most of us live and work . . . Has there ever been, in all of recorded history, a civilisation whose culture was at odds with the values and ideals of that civilisation itself?[4]

The 1987 General Election gave practical evidence of the truth of Irving Kristol's claim: 43 per cent voted Conservative; even 25 per cent of unemployed people voted Conservative; but only 17 per cent of academics supported the Conservatives.[5]

Many of the values which Conservatives represent, and which are so widespread, are not shared by many intellectuals from the adversary culture. But socialists face this problem in reverse, a much more acute form. They say that they want to help the mass of working people; on the other hand, the liberal–left intelligentsia show no respect for the values and aspirations of working people. It is the fatal weakness of left 'progressive' parties in modern democracies.

The Fabians

The Fabians achieved the greatest shift in ideas on public policy since Adam Smith destroyed mercantilism and put free markets at the centre of a new political consensus. Indeed the Fabians in many ways took the intellectual consensus back to something like mercantilism – they believed in governments organizing economic and social activity with the objective of 'national efficiency' which would be tested in a ruthless Darwinian struggle with other leading power blocs.

The Fabians offered a powerful critique of Victorian public policy and provided an intellectual basis for the emergence of the Labour party. From Beatrice Webb's Minority Report of the Royal Commission on the Poor Law of 1909, to the Labour party's Constitution of 1918, to the Beveridge Report of 1942 and the nationalization programme of Attlee's government, they had an extraordinary influence on public policy because they were better informed and more self-assured than any other group.

The Fabian view of the world is described very well in Shirley Letwin's illuminating essay on them, *The Pursuit of Certainty*.[6] It can be summarized in four positions. First, an almost religious faith in the applicability of science to political and social questions. Secondly, the belief that the technocratic expert could reach the objectively right solution to problems. Thirdly, a belief that as societies became more complex, so they required central planning to avoid collapsing into chaos. Fourthly, a wariness of the checks and balances of normal democratic politics which enabled vested interests to stand in the way of rational solutions. These propositions will be looked at in turn.

We have already seen how the Bloomsbury Group gave complete sovereignty to the individual and his own experiences – nothing should trammel the individual pursuit of authentic, aesthetic, emotional and sexual experience. The Fabians responded to the religious doubts of the end of the Victorian era in a different way – by faith in science and love of impersonal humanity. As Beatrice Webb confided to her diary on 28 February 1930: 'I long to rid myself of my personality – and having all my strivings after knowledge and kindliness transformed into some movement of the ether, into pure intellect and impersonal love.'[7]

The Fabians made ambitious claims for their work as 'scientific' – something they had in common with Marxists. But they had no real interest in the philosophy of science nor any grasp of what scientific discovery was really like. For them, scientific method meant piling up a confused heap of facts on which they rested ambitious policy conclusions. They never addressed the question, to what extent policy recommendations can simply be derived from empirical observations – how you move from 'is' to 'ought' statements.

They did not see that people might reach different conclusions from the same agreed facts. This was the basis for their second proposition – that more and more decisions should be taken by rational, well-informed administrators whose conclusions would be so obvious that nobody would want to disagree with them. Old-style politics would disappear in the face of the compelling results of social investigation. The social researcher would have the same sort of unquestioned authority as the scientist wearing a white coat in a soap powder advertisement who shows conclusively that there is only one soap powder which can remove beetroot stains – it was just as obvious to them that the national minimum wage was the way to eliminate poverty.

The Fabians saw their approach as much superior to the unplanned, haphazard, piecemeal social reform movement in Victorian times. Instead of appreciating the enterprise of individual reformers such as Florence Nightingale, Octavia Hill and Josephine Butler, they stressed planning and uniformity. Victorian philanthropy was to become the province of the state. What the Fabians did not grasp was the importance of variety and experiment in social policy, just as in the wider economy. They did not foresee the criticism that their model of the welfare state was unresponsive and bureaucratic.

The Fabians also assumed that there would be a dispassionate, uncorrupt, administrative élite able to carry out their programme. There is an irony here which seems to have escaped them: the big improvement in the standards of public administration in the Victorian period which gave people such faith in impartial administrators depended on the state disengaging from large-scale economic regulation. Limited government is much more likely to be uncorrupt government. Apart from the more obvious problems of corruption and inefficiency, it never for one moment seems to have occurred to the Fabians that the public sector would itself constitute a powerful vested interest.

Nor did the Webbs consider from what the authority of these bureaucrats would derive – apart from a general respect for science. As one friend observed of them: 'Neither was by temper, instinct or training, democratic. Sidney was a born bureaucrat; Beatrice a born aristocrat. In each case the impulse was benevolent and entirely disinterested; in neither egalitarian.'[8] They thus laid the basis for the distinctive character of the British public sector, that mixture of social deference and socialism which has kept it going over the years. As Chesterton observed: 'Mrs Webb orders about the citizens of the State as if they were the servants in her kitchen.' The Fabians had no sympathy with the Nonconformist tradition of working-class self-help, wary of the state as a further vehicle for middle-class control over their lives. Independent working-class organizations such as the Friendly Societies were amongst the first victims of the expansion of the welfare state under the influence of the Fabians early in the century. They were not interested in political or economic pressures to ensure consumer power over welfare services.

The third crucial Fabian proposition is that as modern social organisms become more complicated, they require greater central organization to avoid anarchic disintegration. Their ideal modern organization would be the control panel of an advanced power station with a small number of technicians watching the dials and running the system. This led them to miss completely the importance of nationalism and independence movements. They saw them as essentially reactionary because they believed the future lay in large organizations – the British Empire was a model of the future.

They were right, of course, about the greater complexity of modern life but completely wrong to assume that this pointed to bigness and centralized organization. It is precisely the increasing complexity of modern life which makes centralized organization

impossible. The information needed to co-ordinate hosts of individual decisions cannot possibly be centrally collected and
then acted on rationally. The market, operating within the rule
of law, is the only effective instrument for co-ordinating the
individual plans of a host of different agents.

Perhaps the most sinister of the Fabians' beliefs was their lack
of interest in democratic politics. This was because of their
assumption that all people would agree on the rational results of
social science and that therefore traditional politics would die
out. Sidney Webb had no interest in limited government – for
him the best government was government which could 'safely and
advantageously administer the most'. Bernard Shaw put it more
crisply: 'The few will organize the many.' There would certainly
not be a need for any of the mediating structures that stand
between the individual and the state. Graham Wallas, one of the
leading Fabian thinkers, looked forward to the day when the
public kitchen would replace the inefficiency of each family
feeding itself.

This is where their thought comes close to totalitarianism. It
is capitalism which creates the space for communities. Totalitarianism and socialism reduce us all to atomistic units, subject
to state control.

It is the intellectual background to their infatuation with
the Soviet Union. As they said: 'Old people often fall in love in
extraordinary and ridiculous ways – with their chauffeurs, for
example: we feel it more dignified to have fallen in love with
Soviet communism.'[9] But they were not alone in their passion
for the Soviet Union – at least two generations of socialists took
it as a model for the future.

The Fabians encountered surprisingly little serious intellectual
opposition from conservatives. The hostility and mockery came
largely from literary circles. Sometimes it was their own as-
sociates who mocked them during disputes – H. G. Wells, for
example. Chesterton and Belloc saw through them from the
beginning. Malcolm Muggeridge remarked that the Webbs
'pursued truth through facts' and arrived at 'fantasy'; they
sought 'deliverance through power' and arrived at 'servitude'.[10]
He saw that these rationalist social engineers ended up in the

wilder reaches of irrationalism. Hazlitt captured the absurdity of such schemes:

> Those who think they can make a clear stage of it, and frame a set of opinions on all subjects by an appeal to reason alone, and without the smallest intermixture of custom, imagination, or passion, know just as little of themselves as they do of human nature ... custom, passion, imagination, insinuate themselves into and influence almost every judgment we pass or sentiment we indulge, and are a necessary help (as well as hindrance) to the human understanding; and that to attempt to refer every question to abstract truth and precise definition, without allowing for the frailty of prejudice, which is the unavoidable consequence of the frailty and imperfection of reason, would be to unravel the whole web and texture of human understanding and society. Such daring anatomists of morals and philosophy think that the whole beauty of the mind consists in the skeleton; cut away, without remorse, all sentiment, fancy, tastes, as superfluous excrescences; and in their own eager, unfeeling pursuit of scientific truth and elementary principles, they 'murder to dissect'.[11]

The Rise of Organized Labour

Not only did the first half of the twentieth century see the erosion of respect for the old order and its rules amongst the intelligentsia, driven by World War One and Bloomsbury; not only did an alternative, seductive socialist programme emerge, formulated by the Fabians; but this period also saw a powerful mass economic and political force which could push the new ideas forward: organized labour.

Perhaps the most powerful images of British life in this period are the flickering newsreels showing large crowds of men – all wearing caps and remarkably orderly – going to a factory, a football match, or on a march. It is the era of the masses, the period of the truly giant factory. Probably the biggest reason for the rise of the collectivist, egalitarian mentality during this period was the experience of mass production. Thousands of people worked side by side on the same production line doing virtually identical tasks and earning the same wage. Equality meant something for them; it was their practical, day-to-day experience. And collective action, through mass trade unionism, was the best way to increase their pay in the short term. Moreover, if life on the production line was grey and boring, this was taken as evidence of capitalist exploitation.

These unionized industrial workers provided the natural base for the Labour party. The figures for the Labour vote throughout this period tell an extraordinary story of almost inexorable increase. They show what the Fabians called 'the inevitability of gradualness'. In 1900 the Labour party won about 60,000 votes. By 1910 it was 500,000 (with a modest setback in the second general election of 1910). By 1918 there were over 2 million, rising to 5.5 million in 1924, and to over 8 million in 1929. A brief setback came in 1931, and it was recouped in 1935. Then, of course, there was the landslide 12 million votes cast for the Labour party in 1945. The rise of the Labour vote, resting on a solid, trade union, industrial base, was the most important political fact of life in Britain during the first half of the twentieth century.

The Conservative Response

The rise of collectivist ideas and increasing state activity prompt some fundamental questions. Is collective action simply an intellectual error, threatening everything that is best in Britain? Or is it an inevitable corollary of large-scale modernization; simply one aspect of modernity? If the former, it should be fought, opposed and driven back. If the latter, the true Conservative task is to accommodate it; to tame it; to anglicize it (indeed, maybe, to use an authentic period phrase, to appease it).

For the first quarter of this century the Conservative party fought against collectivism and in defence of property with almost desperate energy. But the Conservative party lost the argument against a bigger rôle for the state in guiding the economy and financing welfare services. It then became embroiled in a subsidiary argument as to whether this expanding state should raise the money it needed by taxing property or by tariffs on imports from outside the Empire. The party increasingly advocated tariffs which, it was argued, would help domestic manufacturers rather than burden them – as the other taxes would. Imperial preference for the first time set Disraelian imperialism in conflict with the party's traditional belief in free trade. It divided the party by setting two of its principles in direct conflict. The Irish question also put the party under great strain, by again putting its principles in conflict with each other – should it support illegal action in defence of the integrity of the United Kingdom itself? And the Conservatives just did not have leaders of the eloquence and persuasiveness of Asquith or Lloyd George, who might have steered it through the turmoil of the first quarter of the century. Bonar Law did not exactly exude charm and bonhomie. Austen Chamberlain looked like Hercule Poirot.

When Baldwin became leader in 1923 the party's fortunes revived as it moved to a much more accommodating answer to the fundamental question posed above – though it did defeat the General Strike and held to a tight financial policy during the late 1920s. Baldwin's style was to be above the fray: different interest groups might be in conflict but the job of a Conservative government was to reconcile them. He tried to be to political disputes what ACAS (the Arbitration, Conciliation and Advisory Service) is to industrial relations. This willingness to tolerate the collectivist advance was associated with his almost elegiac picture of England; a world was passing:

> To me, England is the country and the country is England. And when I ask myself what I mean by England, when I think of England when I am abroad, England comes to me through my various senses – through the ear, through the eye, and through certain imperishable scents. I will tell you what they are, and there may be those among you who feel as I do.
>
> The sounds of England, the tinkle of the hammer on the anvil in the country smithy, the corncrake on a dewy morning, the sound of a scythe against the whetstone, and the sight of a plough team coming over the brow of a hill, the sight that has

been in England since England was a land, and may be seen in England long after Europe has perished and every works in England has ceased to function, for centuries the eternal sight of England. These things strike down into the very depths of our nature and touch chords that go back to the beginning of time and the human race, but they are chords that with every year of our life sound a deeper note in our innermost being.[12]

Many people think this is the distinctive tone of conservatism before Margaret Thatcher: a party walking into the future, looking back into the past; a party which tries to moderate what was seen as the inevitable advance of socialism, whilst at the same time appealing to a nostalgic, pastoral picture of England.

This Baldwinian view of politics as taming a host of dangerous forces was well summarized by Reginald Maudling in a different context when he said: 'When in trouble with the police, particularly in a foreign country, patience, amiability and an infinite desire to please are the essential ingredients of escape.'[13] It is one rôle for a conservative, well suited to times of turbulence and tension when anti-conservative forces are rampant – as in the Britain of the inter-war period. Baldwin certainly succeeded in outmanoeuvring and outwitting very dangerous forces, from Lloyd George through to the striking miners. But the risk is that instead of achieving moderation, it can encourage extremism. It is the politics of splitting the difference and if that is the game then the best opening position is to establish a very big difference indeed. The political and intellectual initiative belongs to others.

The feebleness of the conservative intellectual response to the advance of socialism is also shown in the development of government policy during this period. As it abandoned its older commitment to free markets, individual liberty and the rights of property, so the Conservative party increasingly turned to corporatism as its halfway point between sense and nonsense. The Federation of British Industry, founded in 1917, by 1930 was the largest body of its kind in the world. All civil aviation companies were merged into one subsidized public corporation, Imperial Airways. The electricity grid was nationalized in 1927. The roots of corporatism and nationalization go back way before

Attlee's government to the activities of Baldwin's governments. As a Conservative Office publication of 1945 pointed out:

> This country was not exactly a jungle before the War. Our economic life was controlled to a far greater extent than any other country except Russia and Nazi Germany. By income tax, super tax and death duties, incomes were redistributed on a scale which by American standards would be regarded almost as confiscation. Hours and conditions of labour were regulated. Farming was organized in marketing boards. State monopolies had been created in broadcasting, London transport, and in the production of electricity. Municipalities were taking an increasing part in housing, transport, gas, water and electricity.[14]

Baldwin's government brought 'both sides of industry' together to discuss economic policy; the granddaddy of many such exercises in tri-partism was the Mond–Turner talks of 1928. They promised as much, and delivered as little, as all future such exercises. *The Economist* was scathing about this corporatism: 'We are within measurable distance of setting up a new feudal system, with a British market, instead of British land, parcelled up among the barons.'[15]

The most vivid and depressing evidence of how much conservatism had shifted since Salisbury's day is Harold Macmillan's book *The Middle Way*, first published in 1938. It was perhaps an example of Macmillan's sense of mischief that he gave his radical tract such a Baldwinian title. The arguments in it would now be regarded as Bennite: it is a prospectus for central planning. The following passage gives a flavour of his arguments:

> The weaknesses of partial planning seem to me to arise from the incomplete and limited application of the principles of planning. The lesson of these errors, which I regard as errors of limitation, is not that we retreat. On the contrary, we must advance, more rapidly and still further, upon the road of conscious regulation.[16]

That one of the party's bright young MPs should argue along

such lines is striking evidence of how far it was moving away from its principles.

And that was even before World War Two, which gave an extraordinary boost to socialist politics from the experience of total war, as Paul Addison shows in his book *The Road to 1945*. The work of the whole nation had been planned by a benign government for morally admirable ends without undermining the fundamental liberties of the British people. It was the Utopia of British socialism. Socialism is a wartime philosophy, and conservatism a peacetime philosophy. In war we are all supposed to be working together to achieve one great shared goal, sacrificing personal desires and values on the way. We accept that our labour should be directed to the place where planners say it is needed. We accept that firms should do what Whitehall says they should. In peacetime, normal civil society reasserts itself. We are not 'Great Britain at War', or even 'Great Britain Limited', but a host of individuals and associations, each pursuing our own purposes and goals but held together by a common culture and common traditions. Then the challenge of statesmanship is to sustain a legal and cultural framework in which people can pursue these projects freely. That was the challenge after World War Two, and one to which conservatism proved extraordinarily well suited.

CHAPTER III:

The 'New Conservatism': Freedom and Prosperity, 1950–1975

The British political scene in the mid 1940s was deeply threatening to Conservatives. A marvellous national victory had been won, but at the cost of socialism gaining its greatest advance yet. Hayek warned in 1944 that Britain was on 'the road to serfdom'. He thought he detected the 'decline of English political ideas':

> The virtues possessed by the British people possessed in a higher degree than most other people, excepting only a few of the smaller nations, like the Swiss and the Dutch, were independence and self-reliance, individual initiative and local responsibility, the successful reliance on voluntary activity, non-interference with one's neighbour and tolerance of the different and queer, respect for custom and tradition, and a healthy suspicion of power and authority. British strength, British character, and British achievements are to a great extent the result of a cultivation of the spontaneous. But almost all the traditions and institutions in which British moral genius has found its most characteristic expression, and which in turn have moulded the national character and the whole moral climate of England, are those which the progress of collectivism and its inherently centralistic tendencies are progressively destroying.[1]

His book had an immediate and dramatic impact. A group of Conservative MPs signed a letter in 1944 arguing:

> We have *lent* our personal Freedom to the Government for the duration – it is vital that the loan be repaid after the war is over ... today the trend of postwar legislation is in the opposite direction. Bill after Bill is being introduced, or envisaged, which involves compulsion and loss of personal Freedom.[2]

Churchill himself was influenced by Hayek's book; indeed, it led him to get carried away during the 1945 election campaign and make his notorious suggestion that a Labour government would soon create a Gestapo. Despite Hayek's pessimism, if there is one turning point in the twentieth century from which the intellectual and then the political revival of conservatism can be dated, it is the late 1940s. It is the point at which a distinctively modern conservatism emerges. Instead of resting on traditional allegiances – however potent – it reached out to a democratic electorate with a principled defence of freedom, and the practical promise of increasing prosperity. These two themes, freedom and prosperity, enabled the party to appeal to an electorate looking forward to the future.

This Conservative resurgence was made possible, in part, by the decay of socialism. The Attlee government's detailed control of the peacetime economy was the furthest socialism was ever to reach into British life. Like the spreading and shrinking of the polar icecaps, the late 1940s were the socialist Ice Age when it covered most of British life and the point from which it retreated in the great postwar thaw. It was a world of queuing and rationing sustained by what was in many ways a most noble wartime spirit of egalitarianism and willingness to subordinate one's own personal interest to a greater goal. But this revealed that socialism was essentially a wartime philosophy, with the government as the general and the citizenry its troops. The politics of peacetime were very different: governments had to provide a framework within which people and organizations could pursue a wide variety of different purposes.

The intellectual counterattack on socialism began from within its own ranks, with writers such as George Orwell (whose *1984* was 1948 seen from the other side) and Arthur Koestler (whose *Darkness at Noon* was published in 1940). Then, Karl Popper's *The Open Society and its Enemies*, published in 1945, argued against the closed intellectual systems of fascism and communism – variety, experiment and initiative were the source of the vigour of the Open Society.

But this period did not just see eloquent warnings of the dangers of socialism, there was a remarkable revival in sophisticated and positive accounts of conservatism. The opening forty years of the century had seen surprisingly few serious contributions to conservative thought. Lord Hugh Cecil wrote a short book on conservatism in 1912, a fascinating period piece which essentially argues for free-market conservatism because it rests on divine law. Apart from this, there are really only Baldwin's speeches with their backward-looking picture of England. (Sir Arthur Bryant, who helped to write them, also produced his own rather syrupy contribution, *The Spirit of Conservatism*, in 1929.) Harold Macmillan's *The Middle Way* hardly counts as a conservative text at all. After the war, the intellectual scene changes. Friedrich Hayek, Michael Oakeshott and T. E. Utley all reached the peak of their powers in the 1940s and 1950s. The Conservative party also had some exceptionally distinguished and reflective politicians, such as Enoch Powell, Iain Macleod and Quintin Hogg – whose brilliant book *The Conservative Case* remains the best account of conservative ideas.

Perhaps the war itself helped to stimulate this conservative thought. World War Two was possibly the most heroic project upon which the British people had ever embarked. It was therefore imperative, yet also very difficult, to explain that this was not what government should be like in peacetime – hence Oakeshott's distinction between the state as an enterprise association and a civil society. It is the distinction between government pursuing projects and government providing a framework within which others can pursue their projects. A rather pathetic plea by Winston Churchill during his peacetime government shows this distinction: 'In the worst of the war I could always see how to do it. Today's problems are elusive and intangible.'[3]

The Party of Freedom

The modern conservatism which gives this book its title emerges after World War Two. It remains true to the party's traditions but has a distinctive character of its own. First, it emphasizes the party's commitment to freedom. Second, it applies the principle of freedom to economic management and shows how that yields prosperity. Third, it accepts large parts of the welfare state, but on sound conservative grounds. These three elements comprise what was called at the time the 'new conservatism'.

Postwar Conservatives saw themselves as bearing the responsibility of being the party of freedom now that socialism had displaced liberalism as their political opponent. Herbert Spencer's forecast fifty years earlier that the Conservative party might become the party of freedom had come true. It became one of the clichés of conservative writing at the time. Harold Macmillan made the point in his new introduction to *The Middle Way*:

> Our Tory party, which stressed the claims of authority (the need for the State to protect the weak) in the nineteenth century, and which champions the claims of liberty in the twentieth century, has not changed its ground; it is occupying the same ground, the middle ground. It is only the direction of the attack which has altered.[4]

Quintin Hogg makes the same point in his book:

> In fighting socialism in the twentieth, as they fought liberalism in the nineteenth century, Conservatives will be found to have changed their front to meet a new danger, but not the ground they are defending.[5]

Conservatives had always been a party of freedom, now they were *the* party of freedom. This had an effect on how Conservatives saw their political responsibilities, and on the nature of Conservative argument. That effect first becomes obvious at the end of World War Two. It is one of the reasons that postwar conservatism is a distinctive movement.

There is a second novel element to postwar conservatism. It is captured in the slogan for the 1955 election: 'Conservative Freedom Works'. Freedom was not just a good thing in itself; when applied to economic policy it meant reliance on market forces which in turn offered the best hope of prosperity. Conservatives were arguing that their view of the world made them best suited to managing the economy. And this appealed to a mass electorate increasingly interested in future prosperity as much as past achievement. Some of the old and most precious conservative institutions – the Empire, the prerogatives of the House of Lords – were disappearing. They carried little weight with an electorate which had come to look on economic prosperity as one of the responsibilities of government. So Conservatives became more instrumentalist ('this is what government can do for you') and more future-oriented ('this is how we can make things better'). Free-market economics neatly met these imperatives of the postwar electorate, whilst remaining true to the traditions of the Conservative party.

Conservatives confronted the dilemma identified at the end of the previous chapter: to what extent was the development of the state in the first half of the twentieth century an appalling mistake or was it an inevitable aspect of economic advance? The Conservative view was that detailed state intervention in the economy was largely a mistake. Conservative economic policy during the 1950s rejected the Baldwinian corporatism of the 1920s and 1930s. But when it came to the welfare state, the third element of the new conservatism, it was recognized to be impossible, and undesirable, to turn the clock back to before Lloyd George and before Churchill's wartime Coalition. Indeed, the party could claim a long tradition of social reform with substantial legislation to its credit. There was a distinctive Conservative case for the welfare state – resting on the principles of mutual insurance and the obligations which we all have to our fellow countrymen (see Chapter X).

This modernization of the Conservative party is associated, above all, with the One Nation Group. The One Nation Group of Tory MPs is one of the most significant movements of the twentieth-century parliamentary Conservative party, and one of the most misunderstood. The conventional wisdom sees it as the triumph of the Tory left, helping conservatism escape from its association with the mistakes of the 1930s. But the founders of the group were actually much less interventionist than the interwar generation of Conservatives. They transmuted the intellectual revival of conservative thought into an effective force in Conservative politics.

Their pamphlet on economic policy, published in 1954 and written, amongst others, by Enoch Powell and Angus Maude, showed the clear change in economic thinking towards free markets. The title, *Change is our Ally*, conveys a clear message about their view of industrial problems. Their conclusion could not be clearer:

> Political thought and practice during the last 40 years have swung away from *laissez faire* toward the opposite extreme of centralised planning and control ... In the second half of the twentieth century the creation of new wealth has become our most urgent need. If this is to be achieved we believe that the pendulum must swing back to a more competitive system ... This means a reversal of the trend of the pre-war era. In the 1920s and '30s, rationalisation, whether under public or private control, was the order of the day. Employers and owners of capital saw in it an insurance against sudden and complete defeat; employees thought that it offered some guarantee against the worst forms of unemployment. The whole emphasis was on the defence of the *status quo* ... Since the war the economic setting has become utterly different ... The emphasis has thus shifted from stability to change.[6]

Their main interest, however, was not in economic but in social policy. Their first pamphlet, published in 1950, set out 'a Tory approach to social problems'. The title, *One Nation*, harking back to Disraeli, was a reminder of the long history of Conservative social reform. This was something on which the pamphlet's authors, despite their wide range of viewpoints, could agree. Indeed, for Enoch Powell, for example, it followed on from the Conservative conception of the nature of the political community. But the pamphlet then went on to argue against indiscriminate expenditure on the welfare state, which was seen as putting too great a strain on the economy when set alongside the rearmament programme and the need for further resources for investment. They argued for liberalizing planning control and the deregulation of the construction industry so that the private sector could take on a bigger rôle in housing. They were

wary of top-heavy administration of education by local authorities and the new host of 'experts' who were deflecting 'the
energies of their pupils from their pursuit of basic knowledge'. It
all sounds, dare one say it, very Thatcherite.

They argued that the redistribution of income had gone too
far and set out the classic argument that too big a welfare state
can alienate us from our neighbours:

> When the State redistributes income and property to give every-
> one the largest amount possible, the citizen who has paid his
> taxes has discharged in full his obligations to the huge benefit
> pool to which he belongs. The State is now the keeper of his
> conscience and duty; he gives and receives exactly what the State
> thinks right. Perhaps this is the millennium of 'fair shares for all'.
> It is certainly the death of human society.[7]

The One Nation Group thus sets out a line of Conservative
thinking which is free market on economic policy, accepts the
major institutions of the welfare state, but seeks reform of those
institutions and a greater rôle for the private sector. And all this
was placed within a sensible grasp of the need for a balance
between the community and the free market:

> To a Tory the nation is not primarily an economic entity. It may
> place political and social ends above purely economic ones, and
> for their sake may justifiably on occasion seek to prevent change
> or divert it. Yet economic change is the normal environment in
> which nations live, and successful adjustment to it is a condition
> of their well-being. In six years of war and six of Socialism this
> important truth was dangerously obscured and overlaid. We
> doubt if it yet claims sufficient attention.[8]

That constitutes one of the classic statements of the Conservative
position. The emergence of this One Nation Group exemplifies
the wider development of modern conservatism.

Economic Policy in the 1950s:
Wets and Drys

The 'dry/wet' cycle in Conservative economic policy begins after World War Two. This may make policy-making sound like programming a washing machine, but the words are widely used and they do encapsulate an important argument. Wets believe in a bigger rôle for government and looser financial policies; drys believe in less government intervention but within the framework of a sound financial policy. The late 1940s saw the triumph of the drys; their energy and intellectual rigour contributed to the defeat of the Labour party and the Conservative election victory of 1951. That approach was dominant in the new Conservative government, despite R. A. Butler's appointment as Chancellor rather than Oliver Lyttelton, a move which dismayed many on the right of the party. The real blow to the dries was when Harold Macmillan became leader in 1957 at the same time as there were anxieties about the recession costing the party the forthcoming election. After ten years of dry dominance, economic policy became wet in about 1958.

Oddly enough, the resurgence after the war of a less interventionist approach to economic policy is associated with the ideas of Keynes. The socialist project, intellectually dominating the first half of the century, envisaged detailed public-sector control of the economy and society as the only way of achieving full employment and prosperity. Keynes's *General Theory*, published in 1936, was a serious intellectual blow to this. It was admittedly far from a defence of the nineteenth-century economic order, because Keynes argued that even a free-market economy could get stuck with long-term unemployment because of lack of effective demand. But neither was Keynes endorsing the corporatist, fascist or socialist remedies to this problem, hitherto the only alternatives on offer. Those remedies all involved detailed government intervention in micro-economic decisions. But Keynes strongly believed in free markets. They just needed to be supplemented with government management of key macro-economic instruments such as interest rates and the budget deficit. Keynes invented the idea of macro-economic policy. As his biographer Robert Skidelsky has shown, such a macro-economic policy was supposed to leave markets free at the micro-economic level. Compared with the theory and practice of economic management in the 1940s, Keynes represented an attack on state interference. There should be much less intervention than the Fabians advocated, or even Harold Macmillan in *The Middle Way*. It was, indeed, evidence of the decay of Keynesianism that by the 1960s, governments tried to reinforce their macro-economic management with more and more detailed micro-economic intervention (pay policies, indicative planning, etc.), the very controls Keynes had been trying to avoid.

The shift from planning to demand management was swift and dramatic. One historian dates the change very precisely to 1947.[9] Harold Wilson's arrival at the Board of Trade in November 1948 led to the famous 'bonfire of controls'. And as the old controls were abandoned, so the incoming Conservative government turned to the more active use of monetary policy. Bank rate was increased by 0.5 per cent from 2 per cent in 1951 – having been fixed at 2 per cent since 1932 (apart from a brief spell at the beginning of the war). This was the first modest step towards what is now the conventional wisdom of Conservative economic policy-makers: that interest rates are their main tool for managing the economy.

The first years of the new Conservative government after 1951 saw a host of free-market initiatives. Harold Macmillan had set a target of 300,000 new homes to be built a year, and whilst this was initially achieved by a big increase in public housing, by 1954 it was private house-building that was booming whilst the public-sector housing programme began to decline. The Restrictive Practices Act of 1956 was an attempt to improve what would now be called the supply side of the economy by strengthening competition. It was a direct reversal of the old Baldwinian consensus that government should intervene to organize industries and create new, large firms. Ian Macleod, as Minister of Housing, backed by his Parliamentary Secretary Enoch Powell, introduced the Rent Act in 1957. Rents for the more valuable houses, and all new rents, were to be completely deregulated. It constituted the most radical attack on rent controls until the 1988 Housing Act. S. E. Finer conveyed the intellectual mood:

> The distrust of the pricing mechanism, widespread in the thirties, has all but disappeared even on the left. Free competition, a dirty word ('cut-throat') in the thirties, both to Labour and Conservative, has already been rehabilitated among the Conservatives, and its merits are attested by numbers of Labour party intellectuals. The rage for bigness – large-scale enterprise – has been followed by an intellectual passion for the small-scale. Even free trade is becoming fashionable.[10]

But the turning point in economic policy came when Macmillan became Prime Minister in 1957 and in 1958 the economy entered a recession. Grants to industry, which had declined in every year from 1951 to 1958, began to rise again. This was part of a general trend for public expenditure to increase as a proportion of total national output – having fallen steadily for the previous seven years. Peter Thorneycroft, Nigel Birch and Enoch Powell resigned from the Treasury over public expenditure control in January 1958 – that date marks the change in political direction.

In the 1950s economic commentators had looked across to the reconstruction of the German economy as a model; the German finance minister, Ludwig Erhard, was widely respected amongst Conservatives. By the end of the 1950s, the fashionable model of modernization was instead France, with its *dirigiste* 'indicative planning'. This seemed to require a much greater government rôle in directing the economy and helping industry. With the particular pressures of the British parliamentary system, the decisions that resulted were rarely rational. In 1960, confronted with the question of where the government was to support a new steel-making plant, either in Wales or Scotland, Harold Macmillan decided, with typical political ingenuity and economic madness, that there should be two smaller plants – one at Llanwern and one at Ravenscraig. The consequences of that decision have bedevilled British Steel for decades.

In July 1961 the government introduced a pay pause in an attempt to reduce inflation by controlling wages. In August 1961 the National Economic Development Council was established to bring together trade unions, industrialists and government to try to improve the growth rate of the British economy. In February 1962 the government set out a 4 per cent indicative growth target. This was a long way from the conservatism of ten years earlier. These sorts of interventions also marked the abandonment of the original interpretation of Keynes's ideas. Instead of being a mechanism for demand management enabling the government to stay clear of detailed economic interference, the assumption now was that demand management could only be made to work if it was supported by detailed economic intervention. This was the difference between the economics of Keynes and what became Keynesian economics.

Conservatives therefore left office in 1964 having taken their first full spin round the dry/wet cycle of economic management. They dried out during their six years in opposition.

The Conservative Party under
Edward Heath: 1965–75

Britain was more badly governed during the 1970s than in any other decade in our history. One of the less successful Conservative governments, from 1970 to 1974, was followed by Harold Wilson's final ministry, probably the most catastrophically bad government of our entire history.

Edward Heath's leadership of the party had begun well. He had taken it back to a much more dry approach to economic management, mocked as some prehistoric 'Selsdon Man' after the hotel where crucial policy discussions were held in 1969. The 1970 manifesto set out an ambitious agenda of free-market reforms, including tax cuts, greater targeting of welfare state expenditure, cuts in public expenditure, less intervention in industry, and certainly no prices and incomes policy. It was a meaty manifesto which certainly counts as more Thatcherite than the 1983 manifesto – and probably even the manifesto of 1979.

Yet, sadly, all these ambitious plans came to naught. Heath's approach to industrial and economic policy was reversed in the notorious U-turns. The reforms which his government managed to push through did not have any lasting impact. It was like a transplant which fails because the tissue is rejected. Professor Dennis Kavanagh's judgement is that: 'Apart from membership of the EEC, the Heath government has probably left the fewest policy legacies of any postwar government, apart from the short-lived Home government of 1963–64.'[11]

The most conspicuous failure was in economic management. The government, elected on a programme of economic reform, left office with a record rate of inflation, a record budget of deficit, and a record balance of payments deficit. And, showing the close links between economic failure and wider political turmoil, Professor Kavanagh points out that of the twelve occasions on which the 1920 Emergency Powers Act has been invoked – usually in connection with strikes – five were under the Heath government.[12] The government was finally defeated in disarray with the miners' strike and the three-day week of early 1974.

This sad failure of the Heath government can in part be attributed to misfortunes outside its control. The death of Iain Macleod in July 1970, after just a month as Chancellor, deprived the party of one of its finest and toughest minds. The international economic scene was terrible. American borrowing to finance the Vietnam War led to the collapse of the Bretton Woods system of fixed exchange rates in 1971. The oil price rise in the autumn of 1973, strengthening the hands of the miners and pushing the world economy into recession, was the final blow. Nevertheless, a lot of the blame must also be attached to Heath's U-turns in industrial and economic policy.

Initially the government had been keen to disengage from support for industry, and had indeed engaged in modest de-nationalization – selling Thomas Cook's, for example. But in February 1971, after Rolls-Royce had gone bankrupt, it was nationalized in a striking reversal of the government's non-interventionist policy. Later in the same year, Upper Clyde Ship-builders was rescued after workers occupied the shipyard. The

1972 Industry Act then gave the government wide-ranging powers to give selective grants to industry – powers which were ample for Tony Benn when he was Secretary of State for Industry in the subsequent Labour government.

The collapse of the Bretton Woods system posed serious problems for all advanced Western countries. But we fared less well than some others because we had no domestic monetary targets to put in its place. The failure of the brief experiment with the European 'snake' in 1972 (a predecessor of the European Monetary System) left the government without any clear financial framework to control inflation. It turned instead to direct administrative controls – with the first stage of a prices and incomes policy introduced in November 1972. This meant that the government had to find a means of co-operating with leading trade unions, so it was in turn obliged to abandon in practice its ambitious industrial relations reforms of 1971. It was the Conservative party's second experience of the dry-to-wet cycle whilst in government, though speedier and altogether more traumatic than the first.

This second abandonment of free-market economics was much more severe than the first because this time the entire postwar financial framework was jettisoned. When the pound was tied to the dollar in the Bretton Woods system, we did in effect have a monetary rule and Keynesian demand management was restricted to relatively modest adjustments to taxation and public spending. That was why the first experience of the wet/dry cycle was relatively mild. Keynes, who had himself designed the Bretton Woods system, would have been shocked by the insouciance with which the British government was prepared to see the system of fixed exchange rates collapse without putting anything serious in its place.

Instead of accepting this financial discipline as effective and, indeed, benign, they tried to think of ways round it. The Heath government thought it had escaped by floating the pound (i.e., allowing it to sink). If the balance of payments was in deficit, then the pound would automatically fall in value until exports were so cheap and imports so expensive that the balance of payments balanced again. The government could stimulate the economy free of any worries about a run on the pound (because there was no parity it was trying to protect) and about the balance of payments (because automatic devaluation would deal with any crisis). But this dangerous economic experiment meant that for one of the few periods in our peacetime history Britain was cast adrift without any proper financial framework. The result was that inflation approached 20 per cent during 1974 – much higher than anything previously experienced in the postwar period. It is the point at which the British inflation problem shifted from being chronic to being acute.

But the failure of the Heath government was not simply an economic failure. There were political mistakes which help to explain the contrast between the transience of the Heath government and the durable reforms achieved by Mrs Thatcher's governments.

First, the slogans of the time – such as 'Action Not Words' and a 'Silent Revolution' – were deeply unpolitical. They were obviously a reaction against Harold Wilson's wordy ineffectiveness. But they suggest a failure to engage the emotions and imaginations of the electorate. Conservatives may believe in the silent majority, but that does not mean politics can be silent, technocratic management. This was a particularly serious failure because it is difficult to press through bold reforms if there is not an acceptance by the electorate that they are needed. Ironically, the traumas of the 1970s led to a popular recognition that we were slipping behind other advanced Western nations – a mood which Mrs Thatcher could then harness. Edward Heath and his advisers understood the seriousness of Britain's problems, but they were ten years ahead of the electorate.

Secondly, there was the preoccupation with reforming public administration. New Whitehall departments were created. Local government and the NHS were reorganized. It was assumed – and it was not a silly assumption – that the government should set about modernizing itself as its contribution to modernizing the country as a whole. But limited political energies were consequently absorbed in redesigning Whitehall structures – leaving the outside world utterly unaffected. It saw the birth of the Public Expenditure Survey Committee (PESC), Programme

Appraisal & Review (PAR), and the Central Policy Review Staff (CPRS) – of which only the first has survived. One of the lessons to be learned from this is that a government with ambitions to deal with important problems out in the real world should not waste its energy trying to change Whitehall first. Improving the working of Whitehall should not be allowed to absorb so much of government's energies as happened under Edward Heath.

There is a more fundamental criticism of the Heath government. Its failure is evidence of what goes wrong if the 'instrumentalist' view of politics is taken to its extreme. Heath's crucial mistake arose from his seeing politics as simply pragmatic problem-solving. If the government was there to deliver certain things, it would try one set of policies; and if they did not appear to be working, then it would try a different set of policies. Politicians were supposed to resemble managers trying different strategies to improve a company's performance.

A Conservative cannot simply approach politics in such a managerial spirit. There is a bedrock of principle on which a Conservative government has to rest. There are indeed limits to instrumentalism. And, applying the approach which T. S. Eliot described at the beginning of this book, it is clear that a commitment to sound money and to limits on government interference in the economy are long-standing Conservative traditions. For more than a decade after World War Two the Conservative party held to those principles clearly and firmly. Wrong turnings were taken at the end of the 1950s, and again in the early 1970s. By the mid-1970s, Conservatives had lost sight of their key principles and it took Mrs Thatcher to remind the party of them. But it is to do the party a great disservice to imagine that rediscovering those truths meant rejecting the entire history of postwar conservatism.

CHAPTER IV
Thatcherism

The term 'Thatcherism' was first coined by left-wing critics. No Conservative, not even Mrs Thatcher herself, can be entirely comfortable with the term because it implies that the view of the world which she represents is highly personal, even idiosyncratic. It ignores the rôle of other leading Conservatives, notably Sir Geoffrey Howe, Lord Joseph, and Nigel Lawson in developing the policies now called Thatcherism. It also implies that a clique of free-market ideologues managed in the mid-1970s to launch a coup and capture control of the Conservative party. But the previous chapters have established two clear propositions which show how false is the implied antithesis between Thatcherism and conservatism.

First, there has always been a strong free-market element in conservatism, going right back to Edmund Burke himself. Second, Conservatives have always understood that there is more to life than free markets – the ties of history, community and nationhood. Those two propositions remain as true of the Conservative party in the 1980s and the 1990s as throughout its history. Mrs Thatcher may have expounded those principles with a rare conviction and emotional force, and thus given them a distinctive personal tone, but it was still conservatism which she was expounding.

Critics cite one notorious statement by Mrs Thatcher – 'there is no such thing as society' – to support their claim that she is not a true conservative but just a narrow capitalist individualist. But that bald remark is a caricature of her true beliefs, as the full quotation shows:

> I think we've been through a period where too many people have been given to understand that if they have a problem, it's the government's job to cope with it. 'I have a problem, I'll get a grant.' 'I'm homeless, the government must house me.' They're

casting their problem on society. And, you know, there is no such thing as society. There are individual men and women, and there are families. And no government can do anything except through people, and people must look to themselves first. It's our duty to look after ourselves and then, also, to look after our neighbour. People have got the entitlements too much in mind, without the obligations. There's no such thing as entitlement, unless someone has first met an obligation.[1]

Reading the full text of the 1987 interview, it is clear that all she meant was that we could not evade personal responsibility for our actions by saying everything we did wrong was really society's fault. And if we want 'government' or 'society' to do something, that means putting a duty on other people and collecting taxes from them. But Mrs Thatcher did not mean that we had no responsibilities to others, or could lead any meaningful existence outside society. Indeed, one of her preoccupations was with reconciling the world of economic calculation with our moral obligations to our fellow-citizens. For her that reconciliation was achieved through her strong sense of religious obligation. (In her speech to the General Assembly of the Church of Scotland in May 1988 she spoke 'personally as a Christian' and said: 'Most Christians would regard it as their personal Christian duty to help their fellow men and women'.) This question of reconciling economic calculation and social duty is one to which we return in Chapter VII.

Nevertheless there was, of course, a lively argument about the true direction for conservatism throughout Mrs Thatcher's leadership. It was the battle between dry and wet which the previous chapter shows had really gone on throughout the postwar period, though the terms only appear in the early 1980s. The last chapter roughly outlined the swings between dry and wet in the Conservative party – dry dominance 1948–58, wet 1958–65, dry during 1965–71, and wet for 1971–5. However crude this may seem, and whatever particular exceptions one can cite, it remains a useful account of the party's approach to economic and industrial policy, which now constitutes a benchmark of any party's political philosophy.

It can be seen as an argument about how the party should modernize, faced with a mass electorate swayed by the promise of increasing prosperity. The wets saw French-style indicative planning and co-operation between government, employers and trade union leaders as the modern way of running the economy. The drys put much more stress on the German experience after World War Two and advocated sound money and not interfering in business decisions.

It suggests a deeper pattern to Conservative politics since World War Two. In opposition the party returns to its roots and its traditional view of the limited rôle for government in economic management. And it is the energy and political conviction associated with that which generates the energy to drive Labour from office. Indeed, the Conservative party has only won one postwar election with a looser, more interventionist policy (1959).

Once in office, it proves difficult to stick to the old clear certainties if the economy goes into recession. That is when the government comes under maximum pressure to intervene more in the economy, and it succumbed in 1958 and 1971. The significance of Mrs Thatcher was not simply that she came to power pledged to hold inflation down and intervene less – that was equally true of the new Conservative governments of 1951 and 1970. The difference with Mrs Thatcher was that she stuck to these certainties through the recession of the early 1980s. John Major has similarly remained resolute as Chancellor and then Prime Minister through the recent recession. The party's dangerous flirtation with corporatism and loose money is now finally over.

This is not just an intellectual victory won within the Conservative party. It ties in with deeper changes in the aspirations of the electorate. More young people voted Conservative in the general elections of 1983 and 1987 – an exceptional achievement for the Conservative party, whose support tends to come from older people.[2] The rhetoric of freedom and of making one's own way in the world without pettifogging government control matches popular aspirations. There is a learned debate amongst political scientists about the extent to which popular values changed during the 1980s. Many have not. We still support the welfare state, for example, and quite rightly so. But the one change which has occurred is the aspiration of an increasing number of young people to be self-employed or to set up their own business. The language of free markets and enterprise has modernized the party and left socialists clinging to the wreckage as their ideology sinks beneath the waves.

The Origins of Thatcherism

The triumph of Thatcherism can be traced back to developments in the 1960s and 1970s, both within the party and across the country. The spirit of the 1960s played a part in the success of Thatcherism. This might seem an unusual claim – the spirit of Woodstock is rather different from the spirit of Grantham. The connection lies in the Conservative party's position as the party of freedom and free enterprise. There is a link between the 1960s and the 1980s boom in small businesses – particularly advertising, retailing and design. The entrepreneur is often a rebel who does not want to fit into the large anonymous organization and instead wishes to make his own way in the world. But whereas in the 1960s that preoccupation with the pursuit of freedom and personal fulfilment was frittered away, during the 1980s the same instincts were channelled much more constructively into self-employment and new business ventures. Our internationally successful pop video industry is what is created when Grantham meets Woodstock. Whereas in the 1960s Labour appeared to be the party of innovation, that is clearly now a quality represented by the Conservatives.

The 1960s' counter-culture also influenced the Conservative critics of the welfare state. Conservatives have always been worried that too big a welfare state would be inefficient and impersonal, and could threaten our sense of personal obligation to others. That sort of anxiety, which can be found in the writings of the One Nation Group during the 1950s, is not totally different from that expressed by some later critics of the welfare state on the radical left such as Ivan Illich. Although their conclusions were very different, critiques of the welfare state from both left and right argued that it had been captured by middle-ranking bureaucrats who were stifling innovation and experiment. That analysis provided the impetus for the reforms in education and health on which the government embarked at the end of the 1980s.

The trauma of the 1970s also played its rôle in the emergence of Thatcherism. The political scientists coined two terms to describe the political crisis which emerged in these years. Government was 'overloaded' with more tasks than it could competently carry out. It encouraged the electorate in exaggerated expectations of government's capacity to solve problems and then perpetually disappointed those expectations. Promising too much and delivering too little was a poor base for sustained democratic politics. The other problem was 'ungovernability' – the power of vested interest groups, notably but not solely the trade unions, to obstruct a government and, indeed, defeat it. This obvious weakness of government reinforced the electorate's scepticism as to whether any promises which politicians made could be kept.

Mrs Thatcher's Conservative party showed how these two problems, of overload and ungovernability, were related. By trying to do too much, governments ended up achieving very little. More did indeed mean less. Rebuilding the authority and effectiveness of government required limiting its areas of responsibility and changing the electorate's expectations of government. The success of that strategy was most vividly shown in Mrs Thatcher's ability to survive despite three million unemployed, which all the pundits predicted was politically impossible. The message that governments could not guarantee levels of employment reached home to the electorate. The best measure of her success in dealing with the problems of the 1970s was that by the late 1980s her government was being criticized for the opposite faults – shirking responsibility for industrial and social issues where it ought to act (one might call it 'underload'), and for being bossy and authoritarian ('over-governing'). These arguments are looked at more closely in Chapters IX, X and XI.

So What Does Make Thatcherism Special?

It has so far been argued that the Thatcherite principles of free markets aligned with a strong sense of community are fundamental conservative principles. Those who try to identify what is singular about Thatcherism by presenting it as the rejection of traditional conservatism are, quite simply, wrong. But one can understand why they think this – there was indeed something unusual about Thatcherism. What does make it special? We will not capture that special quality by analysing Mrs Thatcher's actual political beliefs – very little of what she said could not have been found in a typical One Nation Group pamphlet of the 1950s. Instead, we have to look at Thatcherism along a different dimension – as a very personal *style* of politics and *tone* in political debate. Looked at in this way, it can be seen that Mrs Thatcher as Prime Minister possessed a distinctive combination of three political qualities.

First, there is the energy, conviction and sense of battling against the odds which come from seeing oneself as an outsider. As a woman, Mrs Thatcher was never fully absorbed into the club-like atmosphere of parts of the Conservative party. Most of the ministers who had served in Edward Heath's cabinet did not support her in the February 1975 leadership election. As a result, she tended to see herself as a fighter against doubters, sceptics and downright enemies. Whilst Mrs Thatcher as Prime Minister did have a sense of humour, she did not have any sense of irony, any capacity to detach herself from the position she was in. This formidable energy, given direction and purpose by a clear sense of right and wrong, was the source of her greatest achievements: turning round a desperately weak economy, regaining the Falkland Islands, defeating the miners' strike, and successfully pressing for a genuine 'internal market' within the European Community.

But there are areas of public policy where open hostility to people who may oppose one's policies is not so suitable. One may think some trendy teachers or union activists in the Health Service are pretty tiresome. But a government trying to press reform on reluctant teachers or doctors or nurses is unwise to present itself as fighting a battle against what it claims are at best the forces of ignorant obstruction, and at worst the forces of evil. The conflicts caused by such an approach gave rise to the belief that somehow Mrs Thatcher was trying to destroy the welfare state when she was not. The social policy reforms of the Thatcher governments were sensible and necessary, but getting them through required a different approach to politics than that for which Mrs Thatcher was temperamentally suited.

A second distinctive quality that goes to make up Thatcherism is the ability to move easily between the general principle and the practical example: the strategic objective and the tactical decision. This is a political skill suited for both good government and for good oratory. It meant that, faced with relatively narrow and technical decisions, Mrs Thatcher had an unerring ability to tie them in to general conservative principles. She had no taste for long papers on grand strategy, but she very well understood how each individual decision which she took added up to a strategy. This is also a rhetorical skill – the ability to illuminate a grand principle with a personal, down to earth example and to draw a lesson from a particular story. It was shown in another passage in the interview with *Woman's Own* quoted earlier:

I remember going round a housing association home and one lady proudly showed me the fitted carpet in her flat. 'My son treated me to that. He's doing very well. Aren't I lucky?' Yes, and he couldn't have done it if he hadn't worked hard, and yes, for money! There's nothing wrong with having a lot of money. It is not the fact of having money that is wrong, it is when it becomes the sole and the only thing in your life.

This was the source of her ability to cut through humbug and speak with such refreshing openness, saying what we knew to be true but people were not supposed to say.

The third quality was her ability to decide on which issues to fight. This is particularly important for a Conservative because Conservatives do have a general suspicion that things could well be getting worse. It is the spirit of Horace: 'Our parents' age (worse than our grandparents') has produced us, more worthless still, who will soon give rise to a yet more vicious generation.' But the general belief that things are going to pot is not much of a guide to action. On its own it can come close to neurosis. A

Conservative needs to ask two questions about the changes going on around him: Are they for better or for worse? Can we do anything about them anyway? It is obvious that answers are required to those two questions before it is worthwhile trying to do anything.

The difference between Mrs Thatcher and, say, Enoch Powell is that she had an uncanny ability to judge what ground to fight on, whereas he had not. It is reported that in the early 1950s Powell presented to Churchill a plan for recapturing India, leaving Churchill totally bemused. Imagine what would have happened if Mrs Thatcher had decided in, say, 1979 that trade union power was too strong to reverse and she should put all her energies into repealing the 1960s legislation on abortion and homosexuality. Sifting through the changes in British society in the 1960s and 1970s she unerringly identified the ones which cried out for government action and those which should be left alone.

Thatcherism in Practice

We are used to a picture of Thatcherism as the ruthless and singleminded implementation of a narrow ideology. Many of Mrs Thatcher's critics – and some of her supporters – pander to this by attributing to her some pretty bizarre views. It is as if they are playing a new parlour game in which whoever completes the sentence 'If you are a true Thatcherite then you must believe in . . .' with the wildest assertion is the winner. Thus one is told that a true Thatcherite would allow all of the south-east of England to be concreted over, swamp the BBC with advertising, legalize heroin, or ban left-wing plays.

One reply to this argument has already been developed. Thatcherism is within the mainstream of conservative philosophy. The emphasis on free markets and our identity as members of a community are the crucial themes in conservative thought. (Calling it an ideology is simply a term of abuse, though it certainly does constitute a view of the world.) And more specific claims, such as the importance of monetary growth as a cause of inflation, are no more ideological than believing that inflation is caused by wage increases and can be controlled by a prices and incomes policy.

There is a second, more specific reply. It is simply that if you look at Thatcherism in practice, it is clear that it was pursued with a lot of political skill; she did not practise politics as if it were the Charge of the Light Brigade. Whilst Mrs Thatcher obviously stayed true to fundamental conservative principles throughout her period in office, there was more variety and flexibility in her approach than is sometimes recognized. She was much truer to Burke's dictum of the importance of circumstances to policies than her critics, or even some of her supposed supporters, concede:

> I cannot stand forward, and give praise or blame to anything which relates to human actions, and human concerns, on a simple view of the object, as it stands stripped of every relation, in all the nakedness and solitude of metaphysical abstraction. Circumstances (which with some gentlemen pass for nothing) give in reality to every political principle its distinguishing colour, and discriminating effect. The circumstances are what render every civil and political scheme beneficial or noxious to mankind.[3]

A review of the three distinct phases of Mrs Thatcher's premiership shows how apposite Burke's observation is.

The period from Mrs Thatcher becoming Prime Minister in 1979 through to the landslide election victory of 1983 constitutes what one might regard as the 'heroic' phase. The government's agenda was, above all, economic. The task was to stabilize the public finances and bring down the rate of inflation. Ministers sounded like austere bank managers rebuking someone with a large overdraft for living beyond their means. The message was that we had to tighten our belts and the regrettable suffering caused by high unemployment was the result of past overmanning and the world recession. As a political exercise in changing people's perception of the nature of government obligations in economic management, this was remarkably successful.

The economic policies of the time were called 'monetarism' (for a more detailed discussion, see Chapter IX). Monetarism emphasized the importance of financial policy in the defeat of inflation, rather than the pay and price controls of the 1960s and 1970s. The commentators sometimes suggest that no sensible political party should have allowed itself to fall a prey to such economic purism. On the contrary, the Conservative party's rediscovery of monetarism in the late 1970s was a shrewd political move. The Heath government had collapsed because it could not make its pay and price controls stick without the co-operation of the trade unions. The Labour party could much more credibly promise co-operation between government and trade unions in the management of the economy. Any economic theory therefore which made pay and price control the best way to limit inflation put the Conservative party at a political disadvantage compared with Labour. Monetarism enabled the Conservative party to promise it could hold down inflation without having to get embroiled in detailed negotiations with trade unions. It was not only sensible economics, it was crucial to the political recovery of the party from the debacle of 1974.

It also enabled the Conservative party at last to embark successfully on trade union reform, widely seen to be essential to Britain's industrial recovery. No government which looked to trade union co-operation in controlling pay was going to be able to reform them as well. Monetarism broke that union veto. In the mid-1970s the absence of a close link between the Conservative party and trade unions was seen as a problem – both politically and in economic management. Ten years later, the real problem was understood to be exactly the opposite: the Labour party's dependence on trade unions. This shift in perceptions was of critical political importance.

Sir Geoffrey Howe's 1981 budget has achieved almost mythical status as the moment when the government rejected the postwar consensus and tightened policy although we were at the bottom of a recession. The subsequent growth of the economy in the summer of 1981 vindicated his judgement. That is true so far as it goes, but the reality was rather more complicated. Sir Geoffrey Howe and Nigel Lawson (then Financial Secretary to the Treasury) wanted to reduce the budget deficit so as to make it possible to cut interest rates whilst keeping to a sound financial policy. The tightening of fiscal policy was balanced by a loosening of monetary policy during the winter of 1980–81, with big cuts in interest rates.

The revival of the economy after 1981 was the basis for an improvement in the Conservatives' electoral fortunes which preceded the Falklands conflict. That reinforced the perception of Mrs Thatcher's strength of character. But it also tied in directly to the success of her economic policies. One contrast with Suez was that we had American co-operation, instead of American obstruction. A second contrast with Suez was that because of the government's sound financial policies, with a firm exchange rate and a small budget deficit, the markets remained solid throughout the crisis. It was a reminder of one of the oldest lessons from Britain's overseas wars – that sound public credit was essential to prosecute them successfully. Supposedly newfangled monetarism was actually the traditional basis for successful pursuit of Britain's interests abroad.

The Prime Minister did not send a task force against every problem. Occasionally discretion was the better part of valour. Expensive promises were made during the 1979 election campaign – for example, to raise public-sector pay – which had to be honoured, and made it much more difficult for the government to get public expenditure under control in its first years. And when the South Wales miners threatened to go out on strike in 1981 over pit closures, the government backed down. Although there were occasional reviews of aspects of the welfare state, these were never seriously pursued either.

One policy which has since become one of the central themes of Thatcherism hardly emerged until the end of her first government – privatization. It is an interesting example of how Mrs Thatcher and her ministers did not retreat in the face of difficulties but, instead, advanced further. They did not start as radicals but their experiences made them so. The government's initial approach after being elected in 1979 was simply to promise to manage The nationalized industries better than the other political parties could. The nationalized industries were to be freed from political intervention in commercial decisions. But it slowly became clear that if the government owned an industry, then ministers could not help but be involved in a host of decisions about it. And whilst the nationalized industry management might want to be in a limbo, freed from both normal commercial pressures and also from political pressures, there was no reason why anyone should grant them such remarkable autonomy. If they wanted to raise private finance free from Treasury control, and to decide their own investment without having to go to the Treasury for approval, then they had to be genuinely in the private sector. By 1983 the government was committed to privatizing British Telecom – after a cautious experiment with the so-called Buzby Bond to enable BT to raise private finance whilst remaining in the public sector had collapsed through its own internal contradictions.

By 1983 ministers could feel they had achieved a lot. Many of the crucial objectives which the government had set for itself in 1979 had been achieved: inflation was down; prosperity was rising; the government's trade union reforms were beginning to have an effect; and the Falklands War began to remove the fear that after Vietnam, Western democracies would be incapable of using military force, however just the cause. The 1983 election was a walkover.

The manifesto for the 1983 election was bland and vague. Those who imagine that Mrs Thatcher believed in some sort of Maoist permanent revolution will find their views refuted by that anodyne document. There was a real risk that the government would run out of steam during its second term in office. This gap was filled by the activity of a socialist opposition based in the trade unions and local government which dominated the second phase of Mrs Thatcher's government. Left-wingers had not believed that Mrs Thatcher would survive for long and were angry to find themselves in a parliamentary minority. Some argued that this meant that there had to be extra-parliamentary opposition to the government. Arthur Scargill of the National Union of Miners (NUM), and Ken Livingstone of the Greater London Council (GLC) were only too keen to oblige. Thus the government found itself for the next few years bogged down in long and difficult battles. They were, in a way, dealing with problems left over from the Heath government.

It was during the 1970s that the miners had gained the power to drive the government from office. That power had to be broken. The author recalls how meetings at Downing Street during the miners' strike on any other subject were quite likely to be interrupted by more news on the miners' strike. It was like a scene from one of Shakespeare's history plays with messengers rushing in to announce that: 'Nottinghamshire is with us'; 'Yorkshire is in rebellion'; 'the Men of Kent are gathering'. The battle to defeat Arthur Scargill's militants was worth fighting. It was a real achievement for Mrs Thatcher's second term.

The government's elaborate cat-and-mouse game with local authorities, leading to the abolition of the GLC, was less obviously worthwhile. The government's increasingly intricate battles with local government did it harm and left the impression that Mrs Thatcher would treat an institution the way a schoolboy would treat an empty can he found lying in the road – give it a casual kick just because it was there.

The problems went back to the fundamental changes to local government introduced by Peter Walker and Edward Heath in the early 1970s. These had destroyed the old unwritten conventions on the work of local authorities. A new generation of predominantly left-wing professional politicians moved into local government after the changes in 1974 and were prepared to do anything which was not explicitly forbidden by statute. The reaction of the government was to introduce new legislation so as to stop local authorities doing silly things. Finally, in desperation, the government was driven to its radical reforms of local government finance aimed at replacing detailed central control with genuine accountability to local electorates who would see a much more direct and simple connection between extra spending by local authorities and higher local tax bills.

The idea behind the community charge was that it was a tax so unpleasant that it would lead local electorates to constrain the activities of local authorities without central government having to do it for them. But the government could be accused of giving local authorities tougher medicine than it was prepared to take itself. There was a striking contrast between the government's proud boasts about the number of people it was taking out of income tax, and its desire to have as many people as possible paying community charge. In the end it just proved politically unsustainable.

Meanwhile, Mrs Thatcher's government had been developing an ambitious social policy agenda to give it momentum through the 1987 election and beyond: the third phase of the Thatcher government. This was a considerable political achievement. Traditionally British governments develop their ideas whilst in opposition and then stay in office until they run out of steam, or do a U-turn and collapse through their internal tensions. Mrs Thatcher's government was attempting in-flight refuelling – a distinctly tricky task. The government was helped in this by institutions such as the No. 10 Policy Unit, the Centre for Policy Studies and the Institute of Economic Affairs which all kept up a flow of suggestions for new initiatives. A distinctively Conservative agenda for the welfare state was then developed. Great services, such as education and health, were obviously going to remain publicly financed but at the same time the challenge was to get the features of markets and competition into the supply of those services. These attractive ideas, discussed further in Chapter X, were distinct from both old-style Fabian socialism and the Heath government's preoccupation with new management structures.

One of the luxuries enjoyed by ministers during the mid-1980s was to be able to think seriously about domestic and foreign policy issues instead of being perpetually preoccupied with a chronic economic crisis. When historians come to compare the detailed workings of Mrs Thatcher's government with those of Callaghan, Wilson and Heath, they will be struck by how, certainly by the mid-1980s, senior ministers had to spend much less time on economic and industrial issues. That is one of the reasons for both the government's impressive activity in foreign policy and its ambitious social reform programme.

The government's success in economic management also gave another sort of impetus to its social policy agenda. Just as motor manufacturers test their workaday saloon cars by driving them to destruction in gruelling African rallies, so there can be few better tests of the basic good sense of a political philosophy than to turn its ideas to reversing Britain's economic decline. Mrs Thatcher's government was elected with a controversial and radical economic programme called monetarism. It was widely mocked and yet, by the mid-1980s, it was clear that it had succeeded both in bringing down Britain's inflation rate and raising its growth rate. That won extraordinary authority for the viewpoint called Thatcherism, and for the government's policies in other areas. The government would not have had the confidence to embark on its radical reforms of education or health or training without knowing that its equally controversial economic programme had been proved successful. And it was the misfortune of Mrs Thatcher's third term that those radical policies were being implemented just as the government's skill in economic policy seemed to be cast into doubt.

Mrs Thatcher's government showed that the Conservative enjoys the luxury of being able to stick to his principles knowing that they also work in practice. A Conservative in government, equipped with a commitment to freedom and to a sense of community, is able to meet people's everyday aspirations – including their desire for greater prosperity. The picture of governments in anguish because their principles do not work in the real world applies to Labour governments; it need not apply to Conservative ones.

PART II:

PRINCIPLES

CHAPTER V:

The Need for Community

Our modern image of the human condition is of a soul stripped bare of all the haphazard ties of place and time, of culture and society – the minimalist figures of a Samuel Beckett play. More banal and popular examples would be the bland universalism of the ceremonies surrounding the Olympics, or the multinational choirs of a Pepsi-Cola advert. We assume that our moral and emotional commitment to others rests on our shared humanity.

This view gets its most influential and sophisticated expression in recent political philosophy, in John Rawls' famous *Theory of Justice*, published in 1971. He asks us what political and economic arrangements we would want if we were choosing them from behind a veil of ignorance – so that we did not know our own economic and social position. Indeed, for the experiment really to work, we have to be bereft of political, religious and moral beliefs – anything which might carry our own identity with us as we passed behind the veil of ignorance.

In such circumstances, which are really the absence of circumstances, it is inevitable that Professor Rawls should guide us to a very liberal set of conclusions. We tolerate an extraordinary variety of opinion, of lifestyle and behaviour, because we have none of our own. At the same time, there does not seem to be any reason for variations in personal affluence; after all, property, inheritance and reward have little meaning behind this veil. The conclusion is that variations in income are only to be tolerated insofar as they enable us to run an efficient economy which raises the incomes of the poorest people. It is the typical world view of the twentieth-century progressive: diversity in everything apart from income and wealth, where egalitarianism reigns.

Conservatives who want a quiet life might settle for much of the Rawlsian argument too. After all, as Vice-President Quayle shrewdly observed, we do live in this century. When it comes to effectiveness in alleviating poverty, free-marketeers can reasonably defend all their preferred policies on good Rawlsian grounds: that in the long run they create greater prosperity, which is enjoyed even by the poorest members of society. So maybe conservatives can safely join this social democratic consensus.

But that would be to abandon distinctive conservative insights which contrast with the liberal contractarian tradition, to which Rawls himself belongs. Liberals emphasize individual rights over the vision of a good life. They think political arrangements ultimately resemble contracts in which conditions are to be met and our rights protected; they do not see them as more like ties of affiliation to our parents or our neighbourhood.

The purpose of Rawls's veil of ignorance, just like all such social contract theories, is to get us to escape from the contingencies of the here and now. The philosophical objection to this project is that it simply cannot make sense. If we pause and ask what remains of us beyond this veil of ignorance, we see that it is a deeply confused idea. Are we to have religious beliefs or not; or not to know? At the very least we need a language in which to think through the experiment; but a language itself is part of a particular cultural tradition with a certain set of values embodied in it. We cannot be Hindus or Christians, English or Peruvian; we cannot speak French or Japanese. In what sense, therefore, are we really persons at all? We are mere ciphers signifying nothing, deprived of everything which makes us different from each other. We are, in effect, identical. As an exercise to generate substantive political conclusions, it is useless; one might as well begin by asking us to imagine that we are sheep. It collapses, like all contractarian arguments, because it asks us to imagine being a person without being in society.

The conservative does not just show that Rawls's argument is impossible – he has a set of beliefs about the nature of the good life. This rests ultimately on an understanding of the sources of human satisfaction. The conservative celebrates and appreciates all those parts of our lives that progressive liberals see as encumbrances. It is all those specific ties to places and people, being part of a culture, which give life its meaning. This is not just culture in the sense of high culture. 'It includes all the characteristic activities and interests of a people: Derby Day, Henley Regatta, Cowes, the twelfth of August, a cup final, the dog races, the pin table, the dart board, Wensleydale cheese, boiled cabbage cut into sections, beetroot in vinegar, nineteenth-century Gothic churches and the music of Elgar.'[1] This culture, described by T. S. Eliot, has a history which shapes us and which we cannot escape. In another of his essays, 'Tradition and the Individual Talent', he observes that: 'Not only the best, but the most individual parts of [a poet's] work may be those in which the dead poets, his ancestors, assert their immortality most vigorously . . . the historical sense involves a perception, not only of the pastness of the past, but of its presence.'[2]

Even our property carries a much greater significance than modern liberals and socialists allow. Indeed, the term 'personality' was originally used by lawyers to refer to someone's possessions. It might be just a vulgar red sports car to them, but to me it signifies that I was the best salesman in the firm last year. And if a beneficent State issued everyone with such a car, it would never mean as much again: the car would cease to tell a personal story. It is not some cynical trick of advertising that makes us associate things with values; culture and personal experience can invest things with great emotional weight. As John Major observed of the tendency to dismiss some crimes as merely 'property crime': 'Tell that to the widow who has been robbed of treasured mementoes of her past life. That's not a property crime. It's a personal wound that can never be healed.'[3]

This understanding of the importance of our ties to a community leads the conservative to value what modern sociologists call the mediating structures. They are the family and the trade union, the neighbourhood and the firm, the club and the church. Burke captured this element of conservatism in a famous passage:

> To be attached to the subdivison, to love the little platoon we belong to in society, is the first principle (the germ as it were) of public affections. It is the first link in the series by which we proceed towards a love to our country and to mankind.[4]

Our identity comes from our language, our beliefs, our experiences, our histories – not all of which can we control. We do not choose our parents, our language, or the place of our birth. And we cannot stand outside ourselves and judge our whole lives. There are limits to what we can reason about.

This conservative account of what it is to be a person offers a powerful explanation of the origins of moral obligations. They follow from the social rôles we occupy. The leap from 'is' to 'ought' (from factual descriptions to statements about how we should act) is bridged by understanding the duties that come with our rôles – father, employee or (most ambitiously and controversially) citizen. These serve both as descriptions of who we are, and also carry with them obligations which we cannot escape. Duties do not come from contracts which are voluntarily entered into but are inescapable parts of our life history as members of a community. This was why Hegel rejected Kant's notion of morality as the decisions of autonomous moral agents which are rational in the sense of being universally applicable. He understood that many moral obligations are not abstract and universal (*Moralität*), but are embodied in particular social relations (*Sittlichkeit*). There are duties such as to our children, to our neighbours, and even more specific ones such as participating in the legal system through jury service. They could not be expressed or understood outside a particular set of institutions or a culture. These are duties which only make sense because of specific social institutions which already exist. We are, if you like, born into them.

Saying that there are limits to what we can reason about, and tying our moral obligations to specific institutions, may seem to come dangerously close to irrationalism. But that would be to misunderstand the point. It is, rather, that conservatives are wary of the tendency to assume that 'reasoning' always means proposing statements of universal validity. Voltaire, the model of a modern man of reason, is reported to have 'made fun of the fact that someone lost a case by the law of one village which he would have won by the customs of the neighbouring village'.[5] That anecdote provides as good a test as any of one's political disposition – conservatives will think it is Voltaire who is absurd. It is because we exist within the particular ties of community and history that grandiose claims to universal truths are treated with such scepticism by conservatives. Conservatives prefer the particular – even the quirky – and the specific.

The conservative commitment to community, as the source of individual identity and satisfaction, stands against a very different vision – one in which the human condition is transformed fundamentally by shedding all such ties. For Saint Paul this is a vision of a Christian ideal in which: 'There is neither Jew nor Greek, there is neither bond nor free, there is neither male nor female.'[6] This Christian idea was secularized by nineteenth-century radicals. They wanted to see a transformation of man in this world. For that required a fundamental transformation of economic and social relations – Marx said he was not interested in wrong in particular but in wrong in general. Now that utopian socialism has collapsed we see the emergence of radical environmentalism addressing a very similar human need. Again we are told that we need nothing less than a fundamental transformation of existing economic and social arrangements.

This spirit of what has been called 'metaphysical rebellion' against the human condition can have enormous emotional appeal. For the conservative, of course, it is nonsense; indeed, dangerous nonsense when applied to this world. It is, for a start, impossible to conceive of such a project – let alone carry it out. Archimedes said: 'Give me a firm place on which to stand and I will move the world.' The conservative understands that there is no such Archimedean point, outside all the ties which constitute our personal identity, from which we can stand in judgement on ourselves and on our society. This is the point behind David Hume's deeply conservative history and philosophy. His *Treatise of Human Nature* is not a study in scepticism but of the impossibility of scepticism being sustained in practice when the philosopher moves from his study.

One complacent suggestion prompted by his argument is that if these radical transformations of the human condition are impossible, then what is there to worry about? Socialists can dream their dreams but they cannot do anything about them. Surely conservatives should devote their energies to worrying about possibilities, not impossibilities.

But whilst the socialists' Utopia may be inconceivable and unattainable, that does not mean that they cannot do enormous damage whilst trying to create it. Look at the tragic seventy-five-year history, now thankfully at an end, of the communist attempt to create 'Soviet man'. Right up until the very end of the USSR, commentators still referred to 'the Soviet people'. There never were any such people. The collapse of the old Soviet Union and its empire has reminded us of nationalities from Russians to Georgians who had been written out of communist history. Real history can begin again.

The critics put forward three serious objections to the conservative idea of community. First, they fear it is dangerously close to fascism because it ends up worshipping the nation-state as the embodiment of community. Second, it has no means of judging between different traditions and institutions – is everything which exists equally valid? And third, we are told that modernity, and particularly free-market capitalism, has made this sort of appeal to shared values deeply anachronistic. These objections will be looked at in turn.

The Problem of the State

The first criticism goes as follows. 'We are supposed nowadays to believe in diversity and tolerance. But the shared and unselfconscious values described above surely require uniformity and intolerance. At this rate, Nietzsche will soon be making an appearance (see below). This is not modern British conservatism at all; it is, rather, an old and nasty sort of continental conservatism in which the nation-state becomes the embodiment of all our values.'

The simplest reply to such criticism is historical. The British conservative tradition is extraordinarily benign and sometimes, indeed, prosaic. As the dominant British political movement of the past two centuries or more, conservatism can claim much of the credit for keeping Britain away from revolution and reaction. It is not a political cause with blood on its hands.

Continental commentators from the end of the eighteenth century onward saw very clearly that England was the model of a civil society. Without an oppressive state apparatus or a standing army, a stable social structure was instead sustained by shared values. Although there were alternative traditions – based on religious dissent and the other countries of the British Isles – there nevertheless was a powerful and unselfconscious set of shared values based on English history, its cultural tradition, its social structure and its Established Church. That was why Nietzsche could argue as late as the 1880s that, unlike on the Continent: 'For the Englishman, morality is not yet a problem.'[7] The belief in shared values which may lead to fascism or communism on the Continent led England to our distinctive vice of social snobbery: the misplaced belief that only our social betters can sustain these values. The aristocracy did in England the job which the state did on the Continent.

But we still need to be clear on the relationship between these shared values and the nation-state. Does the conservative believe in the *community* embodied in the nation-state or rather in an intricate, overlapping *network of communities* in which the nation-state has a special but not a commanding rôle? This question of *community or communities* is not usually presented in so raw a form in conservative thought. It is more a matter of degree than of two exclusive options. But there are different conservative views which can be distinguished.

Burke must be regarded as a believer in the national community. Many conservatives who cite his famous remark on the little platoons assume that they are setting out a conservative vision of a civil society in which the neighbourhood, the family or firm are all valued for themselves. But on closer inspection, the assumptions behind Burke's argument may be rather different. A platoon is part of an army directed by a general towards a particular objective. And he does not actually praise these platoons for their intrinsic qualities, but because they are a means of love of the state. Although British conservatism is not fascistic, can it come much closer to state worship than we would now feel comfortable with? After all, conservatives understand that historically the English people are not citizens of a republic but subjects of a monarch. That monarch is also the head of the Established Church – which pressed for the exclusion of other groups such as Roman Catholics and Dissenters from full participation in English society until at least the end of the nineteenth century. And Nietzsche's remark might be taken as confirming that the British have such a powerful sense of subjection to the established order, that they could not conceive any alternative.

Michael Oakeshott's magisterial essay 'On the Character of a Modern European State' rejects too ambitious a view of the nation-state:

> A state, then ... as it appeared in early modern Europe, was not, one may guess from its human composition, very promising material from which to constitute anything properly to be called a community. The most that might have been expected was that some day, with luck, it might discover some sort of precarious identity and manage to be itself ... And this, indeed, is as much as even the most successful of them can be recognised to have achieved ... no European state (let alone an imitation European state elsewhere in the world) has ever come within measurable distance of being a 'nation-state'.[8]

The 'United Kingdom of Great Britain and Northern Ireland' confirms this observation. There is, of course, a powerful sense of Englishness. But Scotland not only has its own culture and traditions, but retains its own legal system. (What would Voltaire make of that?) The position of the Anglican Church is different in the other countries of the United Kingdom. The Conservative party is not the English nationalist party, it is the Unionist party, a fundamentally different thing. Our union between distinct countries can only be sustained if no one country pushes its own values and institutions too forcefully on to the others.

Oakeshott goes on in his essay to distinguish between the state as a civil association and as an 'enterprise association'. In a civil association the state maintains a framework within which people are free to pursue their own purposes. An enterprise association is one in which the state has its own projects and a political leadership which sees itself as a general at the head of an army. The following passage surely summarizes the true conservative position:

The urge to impose upon a state the character of a *solidarité commune* is certainly a notable disposition but, so far from being the dominant disposition of the modern European political imagination, it is easily recognised as a relic of servility of which it is proper for European peoples to be profoundly ashamed . . . no European alive to his inheritance of moral understanding has ever found it possible to deny the superior desirability of civil association without a profound feeling of guilt.[9]

Perhaps two separate examples of the sense of community in practice will show how intricate it is. One example is the British regimental system giving our soldiers such a strong sense of representing something smaller and more specific than their country. The main infantry unit in the Seventh Armoured Brigade during the Gulf War was the Staffordshire Regiment, of which 90 per cent of the soldiers were recruited from Staffordshire and the West Midlands. One infantryman told a journalist shortly before going into battle:

Virtually all my friends are with me here; I just don't know anyone else from back when I was at school. Most of us come from the same sort of background, working-class I suppose you'd call it, in the same sort of town, so we already have lots in common before we join up . . . Obviously people are wondering what it will be like if we go in; how they'll react to combat. But I honestly think the fear of being shown up in front of other people will overcome that. Nobody wants it to get home that he lost his nerve or did nothing to help a mate who was hit.[10]

Those soldiers were prepared to die for the pride of their regiment, for their country and perhaps, ultimately, for some principles in the international community. A month before that report appeared a film critic reviewed the films of 1990. He observed that most of the European co-productions were of poor quality, apart from two: 'Both films worked because their very subject was disorientation. Strangers in a strange land, undone by alien manners, may be the true and only subject for co-productions in Europe.'[11] We cannot trace the ties of community to one particular institution – one is tempted to say they are more like concentric circles, to be, literally, egocentric about it.

The communitarian vision of the state became increasingly the property of the left during the nineteenth century. The British followers of the German idealists (such as Hobhouse and Green) led the shift in the British liberal tradition away from free markets towards a conception of the state as having paternalistic responsibilities towards all its citizens. This is the background to George Orwell's famous remark that England was like a family with the wrong members in charge – as if somehow a tiresome maiden aunt had usurped the true authority of a socialist paterfamilias. It is an odd and sinister image.

Whatever their view of the state before the transformation of politics brought about by the French Revolution, conservatives have learned through painful experience that big government does not embody a sense of community but threatens it. If our benign and co-operative relations with our fellow citizens become instead functions of the state, then we are indeed reduced to merely atomistic individuals pursuing our own self-interest. And the individual communities and causes to which we subscribe do become engaged in a destructive Hobbesian war against each other if they are trying to capture access to a government endowed with massive resources and coercive power. The modern conservative has to conclude from the experience of this century that the big state does not express our sense of community, but is the major threat to it.

That is why a modern conservative has the difficult task of both valuing community as the source of one's sense of identity and of warning against looking to government and the nation-state as the exclusive embodiment of this sense of community. It is a challenge to which I return in Chapter VII.

The Problem of Judgement

The second line of objection to this conservative emphasis on tradition and scepticism about utopian visions is that it collapses into total relativism. We lose all ability to judge anything. Does the conservative simply think that everything which exists is all right? Conservatives, so the critics say, just 'utopianize the present'. The question of whether or not we can stand in judgement on totally different societies with their own traditions raises deep questions in moral philosophy which need not detain us here. But we do need to face the question of whether or not we can judge between different institutions and practices within our own society. After all, Great Britain has a rich variety of domestic political traditions. The communities, which have to be respected and which give people their identities, include trade unions and left-wing political parties. Radical historians remind us of the activities of the Levellers and the Chartists. Coming from the oldest industrial country, our indigenous socialists do not need to look to utopian visions for their politics; they can be derived from the long history of the British working-class movement.

When Arthur Scargill was fighting against pit closures, he did not use arguments about creating a better society. He appealed to the same sense of loss at the break-up of a community that we feel when, say, an ancient estate is being sold off in job lots because the family can no longer afford to maintain it. Indeed, much socialist economic policy is nowadays essentially the principles of the preservation of ancient monuments applied to British industry. This is surely a deeply conservative, and indeed Burkeian, instinct. What basis does a conservative, respecting traditions and established communities, have for challenging nostalgic Labourite socialism?

The most penetrating criticism of Oakeshott's thought is that we end up unable to judge anything. It is put by Gertrude Himmelfarb in her essay on Oakeshott:

Skepticism is innocent enough, even attractive, in an age suffering from a surfeit of principles and enjoying a plenitude of good habits. One can then rely happily enough on those habits without inquiring into their source, their substance, or the reason for their perpetuation. But when those habits become insecure or fall into disuse, the conservative must look elsewhere for the civilized values he has come to enjoy. Oakeshott is right to criticize the Rationalists for subverting all habits, the good together with the bad. But so long as he provides us with no means for distinguishing between good and bad, let alone for cultivating a disposition to do good rather than bad, we are obliged to look elsewhere for guidance – to invoke mind, principle, belief, religion, or whatever else may be required to sustain civilization.[12]

A conservative must be prepared to judge between different institutions within his own society. Indeed, a large part of the political debate in any healthy society is precisely about which institutions are worthy of respect and elevation, and which are in need of reform. The conservative cannot accept everything, be it legal immunity for trade unions or scarlet uniforms for soldiers in battle, simply because it is there.

What criteria, then, will a conservative use in exercising his political judgement? One obvious test is the extent to which specific institutions and arrangements embody the deeper traditions and values of our society. It is because our country has a principle of equality under the law that special exceptions for trade unions are so offensive. These are what Michael Oakeshott calls the 'intimations' from one's own historical tradition. There are further, more specific criteria.

There is the test of durability. If a convention has survived for long enough, that is not only of itself good reason for respecting it, but it is also evidence that it works. Durability may also be evidence that another criterion – usefulness – is being met. If we cannot fully understand a convention or tradition, that does not mean it is irrational – it may fulfil a purpose we cannot fathom (a point returned to in Chapter VII). Any conservative is very cautious about setting up his own personal opinion against the judgement of generations. Hemminge and Condell rightly enjoin us in their edition of the first folio of Shakespeare's plays: 'Read him, therefore; and againe, and againe. And if then you doe not like him, surely you are in some manifest danger, not to understand him.'

Another criterion, which enables one to judge between different political institutions and political traditions, is the extent to which they rely on coercion by state power. Reliance on legal enforcement is obviously not of itself wrong – any conservative understands the need for a framework of law and order – but at the very least, there has to be a presumption against intervening in arrangements reached by mutual consent. If an institution has only been able to survive by deploying such powers, then there is a real need for it to justify itself.

The Problem of Modernity

The third main criticism of the idea of community outlined so far is that it might be an attractive and powerful vision but its day is over; the world is no longer like that. This sort of conservatism appeals to our sense of nostalgia, not our recognition of the reality of modern life. It is anachronistic when we live in a multicultural, multi-value world, and have to rub along with a host of people with totally different values from ours.

Thus, for example, Alasdair McIntyre, a moral philosopher who has offered the most persuasive account of how we can move from 'is' to 'ought', gives grounds for deep pessimism. His argument is that as social rôles and obligations have become more self-conscious, less and less part of our fundamental identities, so the move from 'is' to 'ought' has itself become much more problematic. Peter Berger asks, for example, whether the concept of personal honour makes sense any more as it has to be set in the framework of a precise social code.[13]

John Rawls himself has made an astute tactical retreat. His latest writings concede that his theory of justice is not a general, universal truth that we would all endorse at all times and places. Nevertheless, he claims that it is an accurate account of what people think in a modern, Western, liberal democracy. His argument is no longer an attempt to transcend the world view of a Harvard liberal; it is now firmly rooted in that position. He is no longer asking us to shed all the fundamental features of our identity which would make his argument universal. Instead, we can keep our identities as twentieth-century people, with our particular language and culture, and from that derive his particular set of liberal values.

The final irony, the critics argue, is that the one force above all which has destroyed this sense of community is free-market capitalism. Perhaps the most deeply felt criticism of Conservative policy in the 1980s was that somehow the commercialism unleashed was destroying the sense of community. That is not a new charge. Thomas Carlyle put it eloquently in the last century:

> We call it a Society; and go about professing openly the totalest separation, isolation. Our life is not a mutual helpfulness; but rather, cloaked under due laws-of-war, named 'fair competition' and so forth, it is a mutual hostility. We have profoundly forgotten everywhere that *Cash-payment* is not the sole relation of human beings; we think, nothing doubting, that it absolves and liquidates all engagements of man.[14]

That charge, that commerce above all destroys the communities which conservatives are supposed to value, is the most significant one facing modern conservatism. Is it perverse for the modern conservative to believe in free markets? The next chapter will explain why free markets are so important and then, in Chapter VII, we shall return to the question of the community versus the market.

CHAPTER VI:

The Need for Free Markets

When challenged with the particularly absurd metaphysical theory that the material world did not really exist, Dr Johnson simply kicked a stone in the road, saying: 'I refute it thus.' That is, by and large, how conservatives have dealt with attacks on free-market capitalism. The critics say that it is all about greed and self-interest, a world in which it is every man for himself and devil take the hindmost. They say it is all about protecting the interests of those with property. Conservatives ask what all the fuss is about – industry is more productive than ever; people are more prosperous and can give more to charity; the government has extra revenue to spend on social services.

The trouble is that such a down-to-earth reply concedes all the high ground to the critics. It leaves people uneasy that markets are amoral or un-British or un-conservative. At best they are an unfortunate necessity, the critics say, but for a political party to place them at the centre of its view of the world is like an architect who can only boast about the quality of the plumbing in his buildings. This unease, and the intellectual errors sustaining it, need to be investigated.

Of course there is more to life, and indeed to politics, than markets. Any conservative understands that, as the previous chapter showed. Nevertheless, markets do matter; and they certainly matter to conservatives. It is no accident that almost all the great conservative thinkers, from David Hume and Edmund Burke through to Michael Oakeshott and Enoch Powell, have been believers in free markets. It is the task of this chapter to explain this strand in conservatism.

The collapse of the Soviet empire and the worldwide movement to privatization and free markets is one of the happiest events of a century which has suffered the grimmest totalitarianism. Communism has now been revealed as the longest and most painful path to capitalism. But still there are left-wing critics who do not understand, or value, the principles on which Western political economy rests. They have much to learn from Adam Smith.

His achievement was to identify two fundamental human instincts and show how, when set to work in a free market, they increased human prosperity. One is the instinct to better oneself. This is what leads us to work, to save, to invest. He saw it as:

> a desire which, though generally calm and dispassionate, comes with us from the womb and never leaves us until we go into the grave. In the whole interval which separates those two moments, there is scarce perhaps a single instant in which any man is so perfectly and completely satisfied with his situation as to be without any wish of alteration or improvement of any kind. An augmentation of fortune is the means by which the greater part of men propose and wish to better their condition ... The uniform, constant, and uninterrupted effort of every man to better his condition, the principle from which public and national, as well as private opulence is originally derived, is frequently powerful enough to maintain the natural progress of things towards improvement, in spite both of the extravagance of government and of the greatest errors of administration.[1]

Secondly, there is the instinct to 'truck, barter and exchange'. It is this which enables specialization of labour to occur. One farmer produces wine and another cheese – because one has steep ground for vineyards and one has land for pasture. When they exchange some of their products, they are both better off than if each had tried to make both wine and cheese on his own farm. The engine of ever-increasing prosperity starts turning as people specialize more and more in particular tasks which they carry out with greater efficiency. Exchange allows specialization which drives the wealth of nations. Self-sufficiency is the sure route to poverty.

These instincts, protected by a legal order which ensures contracts are kept and property is respected, are truly the source of the wealth of nations. The legal order also constrains the operation of the market. It protects both producers (regulating conditions of work, for example) and consumers (by banning sale of dangerous goods, fraud, etc.) Such rules are an entirely legitimate part of the functioning of a market. A 'free' market is not completely untrammelled, any more than a 'free' man is outside all law and discipline.

Smith did not call his economic theory capitalism (that term was coined by socialist critics early in the nineteenth century); nor did he call it free enterprise (the term coined later in the century by its American advocates). He called it 'a system of natural liberty'. And that conveys his economic philosophy best. He begins with human beings acting freely and shows that, provided there is a minimal legal framework, this does not lead to anarchy and confusion but to a spontaneous, yet properly integrated, economic system. It no more needs an over-arching explicit plan than a thriving forest needs someone to decide what the ants should do and which acorn should produce oaks. Order can be spontaneous; it need not be planned. Indeed, it is beyond human capacity to plan it all or know it all. It is part of us but not controlled by us; just like our language.

Adam Smith's thought is the basis of modern economics. Economics is about markets. At the time it was a revolutionary challenge to the previous body of economic theory called mercantilism – just as Newton and Copernicus displaced the old Ptolemaic system of astronomy. Unfortunately the old mercantilist way of thinking still survives amongst non-economists, because it is as obvious as that the world is flat, or that heavy objects fall faster than light ones. There is a danger that these misconceptions could gain a hold in the newly liberated Eastern bloc. Three closely related errors still make up a depressingly high proportion of everyday economic comment.

The mercantilists believe that economic relationships must take the form of one person exploiting another; that is the first error. They believe that if you are poor, it is because he is rich. Trade, be it domestic or international, is not seen as something of mutual benefit – if one person gains, it can only be at the expense of another. (Radical feminists now try to apply a similar view of the world to relations between the sexes.) If we all produced exactly the same things, in the same way, and had exactly the same tastes, then the mercantilist assumption would be correct. At best, trade would be useless; at worst, exploitive. But fortunately we are all different, both in what we produce and in what we consume; that is why we exchange with each other to mutual benefit. Every schoolboy knows that if I exchange my old pop record for your football poster, we can both be better off.

Adam Smith robustly stated that 'consumption is the sole end and purpose of all production'. The consumer is sovereign – it is an economic democracy in which we all vote with our pounds. But our interests as consumers are dissipated; our interests as producers are much more narrowly focused. It is tempting, therefore, to look at an economic system from the producers' perspective, not the consumers'. Many businessmen, for example, believe that we would be richer if only the Japanese were not so good at making cars and hi-fi equipment. But whilst the Japanese might make life difficult for our manufacturers, they enrich us all as consumers. We are better off if a Japanese manufacturer makes a more reliable and cheaper car than anyone has in the past. The second mercantilist fallacy, therefore, is to look at economics from the perspective of producers not consumers.

The third error is seeing the world as a closed system; a zero-sum game. It is that assumption which leads people to think of commerce as a refined sort of theft. It is the world of a dead-end business which has no new products, no new ideas, and is just slogging it out for a share of a fixed, unchanging market. In this grim world it looks logical to cure unemployment by compulsorily taking some people out of the labour force – normally picking on weaker groups such as the young, the old, the women. This insane policy only makes sense if one assumes all demands are being satisfied so that there is only a fixed amount of work to be done. The excitement of Smith's system is that it is open-ended. Our unsatisfied wants and free trade create an ever-expanding range of opportunities and products. And because it is open, we can thrive without injuring others. Prosperity is not like being top of the class – a position we can only gain at the expense of someone else. Rather, it is like being well-educated – something we can all enjoy.

But while Smith demolished the pre-scientific economics of mercantilism, other more recent challenges to the free-market view of the world will be considered in turn below:

– that the real world is not as Adam Smith described it;
– that free-market economics appeals to our greed and self-aggrandizement;
– Michael Oakeshott's warning on the perils of rationalism.

Is the Real World Anything Like Adam Smith's Theory?

In the two hundred years since Adam Smith published his *Wealth of Nations*, generations of technical economists have slowly drained the blood from the body of his ideas and preserved it in the embalming fluid of algebra. It can now be proved mathematically that under a certain set of strict conditions, free markets maximize the benefit to consumers from scarce resources. This model is called 'perfect competition'. The first term of most undergraduate economics courses is devoted to explaining it. The trouble is that the conditions required for it to generate the right conclusions are very stringent. There has to be a large number of firms involved in any one market so that they are all price-takers rather than able to influence the price themselves. There should be no brand loyalty from consumers; no barriers against anyone entering the market; no transport costs.

The rest of the university economics course then consists of evidence that markets fail to live up to these rigorous conditions. If there is any competition at all, it is at best 'imperfect' (this should strictly be a technical term to describe some forms of markets, but the implied value judgement could not be stronger). The policy conclusion, sometimes explicit and sometimes implicit, is that as competition is imperfect, governments can intervene as much as they like.

J. K. Galbraith, probably the most overrated postwar economist, mocked the obvious failings of the perfect competition theory. He saw the modern business corporation as a big bureaucracy, undisturbed by risk or competition because of the power it exerted over its customers, easily seduced by advertising. Adam Smith's entrepreneur had degenerated into Galbraith's middle-ranking corporate bureaucrat, more concerned with politicking his way up the corporation than with customers out there in the real world. But try telling that to the management of Texaco or Dunlop, PanAm or British Leyland, once-great companies brought low because they failed to keep up with the competition and to satisfy their consumers. It may indeed be that too many people in American and British corporations actually believed what Galbraith wrote about them and thus became so complacent that it was, instead, German and Japanese firms which were the great postwar success stories. The truth is that even enormous corporations are under sustained competitive pressure. Indeed, the competition faced by big corporations is in some ways more intense than that faced by small firms in a perfectly competitive market who can sell however much barley they produce at the going price. There still is competition out there in the real world.

There is a second reply to this criticism of the unreality of pure market theory, associated with what is now called the Austrian school of economics (stretching from Carl Menger through Ludwig von Mises to Friedrich Hayek). This goes back beyond the mathematics of perfect competition to the flesh and blood of Adam Smith's original conception. The perfectly competitive model is static. The free markets of economics textbooks are eviscerated, sterilized sorts of markets with no risk, no uncertainty, no new discoveries; just costs and prices and economic agents. In such a world there are indeed no entrepreneurs – because there are no information gaps for them to fill, or opportunities for them to seize. It is a view of the world captured in the story of two believers in perfect competition walking down the street. One spots a five-pound note lying on the pavement and the other comments, 'There can't be. If there were, somebody would have picked it up.' Such are the blinkers of the textbook orthodoxy. The Austrian school by contrast places the entrepreneur back at the centre of the economic process.

Austrian economists also understand that some of the knowledge which economic agents work on is intuitive; it is not explicit and cannot be written down. It is tacit knowledge – what they cannot teach you at Harvard Business School. This is the sort of knowledge which the Austrian economists understood to be part of the operation of any economy; it was why full-scale economic planning is not simply impractical but theoretically impossible. And it is, of course, also a conservative insight that any member of a community or institution or society knows much more about it than can possibly be captured in any guidebook or textbook.

There is a third argument which challenges the conclusion that the market imperfectionists reach. They often believe that because markets are imperfect, this licenses the government to intervene to set them right. People who will ascribe the lowest motives and greatest incompetence to big firms, will then ascribe the highest motives and greatest competence to big government. But a whole new branch of political science, called public choice, has now developed which shows that government decisions are at least as imperfect as those taken in the marketplace. Governments also act on inadequate information. Their motives are mixed. And within the public sector there are tiers of officialdom at least as preoccupied with protecting their fiefdoms as Galbraith's corporate bureaucrats. So even if a market failure has been identified, it does not follow that a government programme can be relied upon to solve it.

Greed and Self-aggrandizement

Throughout the 1980s we heard another criticism of free markets – that they rested on a base view of human nature, according to which we are driven by greed and self-aggrandizement. We were told that capitalism just meant every man for himself. That is not just the view of the average left-wing intellectual. It is also the view of the worldly-wise golf club bore who patronizingly tells the young man that everyone of his age ought to be a socialist, but when he grows old he will sadly discover that life is tough and ultimately we are all in it for ourselves. No political philosophy with such a dispiriting view of life would deserve to survive. It is certainly not the world view of a conservative free-marketeer. We need to disentangle the muddled arguments which lead people to believe it is – looking first at our behaviour as consumers, then as producers.

Markets give consumers power over producers, whereas in a planned economy, producers have power over consumers. Markets transmit consumer wants and ensure that they are satisfied. Some of these wants may be elevated and others ignoble; the market treats them alike. It will generate supplies of heroin or incense, depending on what it is that we demand. It is value-neutral. It will not impose on us higher tastes, nor will it debase our tastes lower than they already are. Adam Smith observed: 'It is not the multitude of ale-houses . . . that occasions a general disposition to drunkenness among the common people; but that disposition arising from other causes necessarily gives employment to a multitude of ale-houses.'[2] The market is a mirror which reflects back at us our wants and desires.

The left-wing critics of capitalist consumerism will not be satisfied with this reply. They fear that markets encourage materialism. The usual response of an economist charged with materialism is to plead guilty and say: So what? Free market economies have been very successful at generating more and more material goods. There is more to life than that, but material prosperity doesn't do any harm. Whilst we have unmet material demands, there is nothing wrong with us trying to satisfy more of them. And anyway, socialist planning is equally materialistic – just less successful at it.

Somehow the critics of greed don't seem to think that one can be greedy for an elegant house or for fine paintings. Talk about greed is really a coded way of criticizing what they see as the vulgarity of mass taste. Joseph Schumpeter explained this as lucidly as anyone: 'The capitalist engine is first and last an engine of mass production which unavoidably means production for the masses.'[3] It is a democracy of taste. Sometimes we are so cussed we do not want what our 'betters' think we should – perhaps helping to explain the hatred of capitalism amongst so many *bien pensant* intellectuals.

Economic theory explains the belief of the upper classes that they are surrounded by a rising tide of vulgarity; that, somehow, the vulgarians are doing better out of rising prosperity than they are. As a result of economic advance, things become cheaper and labour more expensive. Those who had access to cheap labour have little to gain from capitalist achievement. Schumpeter illustrates the point thus: 'Electric lighting is no great boon to anyone who has money enough to buy a sufficient number of candles and to pay servants to attend to them.' So the really prosperous are caught between two trends. The masses are able to enjoy more of the things which were previously reserved to the few. At the same time, hand-made commodities and direct personal services rise very rapidly in cost because of the increase in wages (there were 300,000 butlers in Great Britain before World War Two). Perhaps it is this which helps to explain the hatred of capitalism amongst that most curious of groups – upper-class socialists.

The argument that capitalism has a debased view of human nature does not just depend on our rôle as consumers; we also need to consider our rôle as producers. Adam Smith famously observed that: 'It is not from the benevolence of the butcher, the brewer, or the baker that we expect our dinner, but from their regard to their own interest.'[4] Is this fair to bakers, brewers and butchers? The local butcher is doing his job for a whole mixture of motives. Maybe his father set up the shop and he is carrying on the business out of family duty. Maybe he likes chatting to his customers and would hate working on a noisy production line, even though he could earn twice as much. Surely, the critics say, capitalist theory simply fails to acknowledge this great variety of human motivation.

The answer is that apart from one or two basic assumptions (such as unmet material wants), modern free-market economics makes no claim to be a psychological theory of behaviour. Individual economic agents have a host of different motives. The point is that they operate within an economic structure which means that they must at least use their resources well enough for their income to exceed their costs. Whatever the reasons for being a butcher, and however noble these may be, he can only survive as a butcher if he earns enough profit to sustain his minimum acceptable standard of living (or can be subsidized by something else that passes that test).

Believers in free markets are no more committed to saying that everyone is motivated by personal greed than to saying that every tennis-player at Wimbledon is simply motivated to win by the prize money. They are in fact driven by everything from pride to wishing to please their parents. But we can say that, by and large, the best tennis comes from matches in which the players compete to win. Similarly, butchers who are trying to win customers, and so increase their revenues, may well be the best butchers.

Ultimately, advocates of free markets are making certain claims about the benefits of particular economic arrangements; they are not making claims about the details of human motivation. In fact, they are not really interested in motives because these are irrelevant to the beneficial consequences of certain sorts of economic organization.

A Calculating World

We have so far considered the criticism of free markets as appealing to base human appetites and low motives. There is another line of criticism, rather more subtle and sophisticated, which takes exactly the opposite track. This is that free-market economics is, above all, about rational calculation. It is a world in which everything has a price and therefore everything can be calculated. No believer in free-market economics can read, for example, Michael Oakeshott's beautiful essay on rationalism in politics without wondering whether it is aimed at him:

To the Rationalist, nothing is of value merely because it exists (and certainly not because it has existed for many generations), familiarity has no worth, and nothing is to be left standing for want of scrutiny. And his disposition makes both destruction and creation easier for him to understand and engage in, than acceptance or reform . . . He does not recognise change unless it is a self-consciously induced change, and consequently he falls easily into the error of identifying the customary and traditional with the changeless ... The rationalist claims for himself ... the character of the engineer, whose mind (it is supposed) is controlled throughout by the appropriate technique and whose first step is to dismiss from his attention everything not directly related to his specific intentions. This assimilation of politics to engineering is, indeed, what may be called the myth of rationalist politics.[5]

Is an economist really like Oscar Wilde's cynic, someone who knows the price of everything and the value of nothing? It is not only utopian socialists but also some Tories who fear that nothing is sacred in the marketplace. It offers us a world of just things and prices. When people, both on the old right of the Conservative party and on the left criticize free-market economies, it is often the reductionist trust in economic calculation which offends them.

The economist must plead guilty, in part, to this. Economics is an imperialist discipline which claims to be able to apply economic calculation to everything; indeed, the most dramatic advances in the subject in the past twenty years have been in the economics of politics, of law, of the family – matters previously thought immune from economics analysis. When cost-benefit analysis is applied to a public policy problem, a price is indeed put on everything – including human life itself. Policy-makers are faced with questions such as how much to spend on improving that road to reduce by one the number of fatal accidents in the next decade. How much should be spent on a drug that will bring someone another year of life? Some people will find the very thought of such questions offensive, because a life is of infinite value. But saying you want both is not the answer to every question, because resources are not infinite. In a world of limited resources, economic calculation is a tool to find the best way of using them. After all, if we spend ten million pounds on a road by-pass to save one life, when the same sum of money could have been spent on buying a drug for the NHS to save a thousand lives, then we have surely been immoral and not moral. This rational, calculating, economic way of thinking can therefore be a tool for reaching a moral judgement about the use of resources.

Indeed, this way of thinking – the economic way of thinking – crops up in the most unlikely places. Ralph Harris even detects it in the Bishop of Liverpool, David Sheppard, who published *Bias to the Poor* in 1983. First the Bishop criticizes the free market because: 'It is not only the inefficient that go to the wall; so do efficient industries which happen to be operating in areas from which the market has shifted away.'[6] But later on in the book, he seems to take a rather different approach:

> There is no more painful matter in Church life than pastoral reorganisation which involves closing churches . . . Yet it is right to go through the painful process of making some churches redundant in areas where the population has drastically reduced . . . If we keep too many church buildings, we trap small congregations into putting all their energies into maintaining the buildings and justifying their existence by running Church organisations to use them.[7]

Ralph Harris comments:

> If we substitute 'coal-mines' or 'steel-mills' for 'churches', we have a powerful vindication of Ian McGregor's recent activities with the BSC and NCB. My reason for recalling these passages is certainly not to mock one of the most attractive leaders of the Church to which I am sometimes proud to belong. It is to emphasise that much of the lofty moral criticism directed at the market economy and its practitioners is misconceived, where it is not plain humbug.
>
> The Church is as much part of the market as the Coal Board, BL, or, say, the brewers (who occasionally close pubs). Bishops have to close churches, not for the fun of it, but because resources are scarce.[8]

But are there to be any limits to this process of rational calculation, this treatment of everything as an instrument, a means to something else? Schumpeter thought capitalism was incapable of defining any such stopping-place:

Capitalism creates a critical frame of mind which, after having destroyed the moral authority of so many other institutions, in the end turns against its own; the bourgeois finds to his amazement that the rationalist attack does not stop at the credentials of kings and popes, but goes on to attack private property and the whole scheme of bourgeois values. The bourgeois fortress thus becomes politically defenceless.[9]

It is to this dilemma we now must turn.

CHAPTER VII:

Markets versus Communities?

Modern conservatism aims to reconcile free markets (which deliver freedom and prosperity) with a recognition of the importance of community (which sustains our values). This is not a new project. It is the distinctive insight of British conservative thinkers, from Hume and Burke through to Powell and Oakeshott, that these apparently contrasting ideas go together.

Some thinkers maintain that free markets and communities are irreconcilable – that free markets destroy communities. Free markets require the free movement of labour and of capital. Unemployed people are supposed to pull up sticks, 'get on their bikes', and move to where the new jobs are. But if people are mobile, does that not also mean they are rootless? What happens to the traditional stable neighbourhood if it becomes merely a dormitory for a shifting and hence anonymous population?

Moreover, the 'little platoon' may be the free-marketeers' obstructive vested interest, a conspiracy in restraint of trade. Many of the arguments with the professions during the 1980s arose because one man's traditional professional standard was another's restrictive practice. It is very difficult to judge whether sensible self-policing to keep out the wide boys has become a cosy restrictive practice to keep out the new boys.

If markets and communities are alternatives, we have to give one precedence over the other. Socialists back their concept of the community over the market (see the next chapter). Libertarians go for the free market.

The rigorous free-marketeer (or 'economic liberal'), without a trace of conservatism in him, will think that this concern with communities is all agonizing about nothing. What matters is giving people the greatest practical amount of freedom; that means markets. People want increasing prosperity, and that too requires markets. He is not worried if markets erode traditional social ties – seeing it as good riddance.

If ties to a firm, or a spouse, or a neighbourhood are more conditional and more tenuous then, the libertarian says, that may be no bad thing. If a business or a marriage is going badly, it is right for people to break free so they can fulfil themselves elsewhere. He sees life as a giant supermarket in which we are free to choose between a range of different lifestyles and values, as well as jobs and possessions. He cannot understand why conservatives put so much stress on irrational brand loyalty.

A conservative understands that, in Quintin Hogg's neat expression, economic liberalism is 'very nearly true'.[1] It offers a host of valid insights into the operation of the economy, but it just will not do as a complete political philosophy. Free markets need conservatism. One reason was sketched out in Chapter V: economic liberals may see all of life as being like shopping (an image I owe to Professor Ted Honderich) but somehow we need an explanation of what we are shopping for, and why. What makes us the shoppers that we are? Economic liberals have fought an admirable and successful battle for our interests as consumers to be given priority over our interests as producers. But that then leaves the question of who these consumers are; what there is to them apart from their immediate appetites; what they are loyal to; what duties they believe they have. An understanding of our position in historic communities is essential to answer these deeper questions.

Secondly, the conservative understands the importance of the institutions and affiliations which sustain capitalism. There may be a universal instinct to 'truck, barter and exchange', but it only generates a modern advanced economy if it is expressed through a particular set of institutions such as private property, a law of contract, an independent judiciary, and legislation to ensure consumers have accurate information. These institutions need to be sustained by ties of loyalty and sentiment. The law of contract cannot rest simply on a social contract, because that begs the question of where contracts come from.

Thirdly, we do not accept markets and the price mechanism everywhere. You cannot sell your children. You cannot sell your vote. The state does not raise revenue by auctioning places on a jury. Royal weddings are not commercially sponsored (yet). The market system is constrained and limited by other values. A pure economic liberal cannot explain what these are or why we hold to them.

The pessimists fear that capitalism could destroy the very values that are necessary for its own survival. Unlike the Marxists who argued that capitalism would collapse because of its economic failure, these – much more interesting – pessimists (notably Joseph Schumpeter and, on some readings, Adam Smith)[2] argue that it will collapse, paradoxically, because of its success. One of their arguments is that successful capitalism requires what sociologists call 'deferred gratification' to yield the savings that make investment and economic growth possible. But there used to be an advertisement for a credit card with the slogan 'Access takes the waiting out of wanting'. The triumph of the consumer becomes also the triumph of what used to be called the appetites. As one visitor said of California: 'I have seen the future, and it plays.' In the words of the American thinker Daniel Bell: 'Fun morality displaces goodness morality. Whereas gratification of forbidden impulses traditionally aroused guilt, failure to have fun now lowers one's self-esteem.'[3] We indulge ourselves now rather than have projects for the future.

The final twist to pessimists' argument is that the free market, having created a cultural wasteland without traditions and communities, ends up having to bring back authority in its most unattractive and crude form – big government. They argue that if a free-marketeer wants a world like the American Wild West, then the government also finds itself sending in the US cavalry to maintain some sort of order. A free-marketeer boasting of liberating the consumer from fusty old traditions and institutions is, on this view, as absurd and comic a figure as a man sawing off the bough of a tree on which he sits. He is destroying the values free markets need to sustain them.

The conservative thus stands between the two errors of socialist collectivism and liberal individualism and, indeed, understands they are mutually dependent. Big government undermines community. Rampant individualism without the ties of duty, loyalty and affiliation is only checked by powerful and intrusive government. It is the link between the extreme individualist Herbert Spencer of Chapter I and the close family friend on whom he had a great influence, the Fabian Beatrice Webb of Chapter II. One can well understand her reacting against his atomistic individualism by turning to an almost religious faith in the state.

These arguments are not just matters of political theory. They are paralleled in the popular clichés attacking conservatism during the 1980s: 'They don't care ... They would privatize everything if they could ... It's just me, here and now ... It's every man for himself ... Conservatives are only interested in what makes a profit, what pays.' And then conservatives were told increasingly that they were also bossy, turning to central government to control us more, with ever more detailed regulation. This unattractive mixture of rampant individualism and intrusive government is what the hostile commentators wrongly think of as modern conservatism. Even if they concede it is electorally successful, they do not regard it as intellectually appealing.

The criticism levelled at the government in the 1980s which was most hurtful, most serious for any conservative, was that by unleashing free-market forces something precious and British was being destroyed. That is not what John Major, nor Mrs Thatcher, nor the Conservative party stand for.

The opening historical chapters showed that the Conservative party has a long tradition of belief in free markets, but has never lapsed into simple *laissez faire*. Mrs Thatcher was no exception. The author remembers a conversation with her in which she criticized the idea of *laissez faire*. She understood very well that we have ties and obligations to our fellow citizens which go beyond simple economic exchanges. She expressed this understanding in religious terms in, for example, her address to the General Assembly of the Church of Scotland which rested on a Christian understanding of our duty to others. But those religious arguments carry little weight in an increasingly secular society. Moreover, many churchmen professed themselves unconvinced by her arguments. Mrs Thatcher's essentially biblical approach raises the question of whether conservatives have any principled reconciliation of free markets and communities outside the realm of religious belief. That is the subject of the rest of this chapter.

Self-interest and Society in the Eighteenth Century

Reconciling the pursuit of self-interest with duties to the community is perhaps the fundamental issue of moral and political philosophy. And even the more topical form of the question – does commerce destroy culture? – was the subject of lively debate in the eighteenth century. Essayists such as Addison and Johnson argued that commerce led to refinement of the arts. Hume himself wrote elegant essays on the subject, destroying the snobbish belief that somehow the industrial spirit was incompatible with civilization:

> Another advantage of industry and of refinements in the mechanical arts, is, that they commonly produce some refinements in the liberal; nor can one be carried to perfection, without being accompanied, in some degree, with the other. The same age which produces great philosophers and politicians, renowned generals and poets, usually abounds with skilful weavers, and ship-carpenters. We cannot reasonably expect, that a piece of woollen cloth will be wrought to perfection in a nation which is ignorant of astronomy, or where ethics are neglected. The spirit of the age affects all the arts, and the minds of men being once roused from their lethargy, and put into a fermentation, turn themselves on all sides, and carry improvements into every art and science. Profound ignorance is totally banished, and men enjoy the privilege of rational creatures, to think as well as to act, to cultivate the pleasures of the mind as well as those of the body.[4]

But there is a deeper philosophical challenge in reconciling markets and communities. It is addressed by David Hume, Adam Smith and Edmund Burke. Their work constitutes the high point of conservative intellectual achievement. They were rational. They did not accept the traditional explanations of how such a man could at the same time participate in social life with others – neither resting it on divine law nor the 'social contract' of Hobbes and Locke. Their task was therefore to explain the basis for our social institutions, our allegiance to government, and our commitment to property rights.

The source of people's everyday anxieties about free markets is that they see the marketplace depending upon competition between people pursuing their self-interest, whereas community seems to depend on the opposite: co-operation between people looking beyond narrow self-interest. The free-market mind is, people fear, relentlessly calculating and questioning. It never respects things for themselves but it always asks what they are for. Walter Bagehot summarized it neatly:

> Modern life is scanty in excitements, but incessant in quiet action. Its perpetual clamour is creating a 'stock-taking' habit – the habit of asking each man, thing, and institution, 'Well, what have you done since I saw you last?'[5]

The institutions and habits of a society seem to be perpetually under scrutiny. We are never able simply to enjoy them. The restlessness of the modern social conscience is a consequence of the restlessness of the capitalist mind.

It is tempting for a conservative to respond to this simply by sitting back and producing beautiful prose poems about tradition and our inheritance. That is certainly an important element in conservative thought. But, as we saw in Chapter III, the modern conservative has to recognize that this is no longer adequate as a full account of conservatism – indeed, it is doubtful whether it ever was. We have to explain the usefulness of the things we value (though they are valued for much more than mere usefulness). A conservative may doubt whether any one individual can fully understand the purposes served by complex institutions; but that does not mean that a conservative maintains that those institutions do not serve human purposes. Burke regarded 'tradition' not as something deeply irrational, but as a way of drawing on the stock of reason accumulated over the ages:

We are afraid to put men to live and trade each on his own private stock of reason; because we suspect that this stock in each man is small, and the individuals would do better to avail themselves of the general bank and capital of nations, and of ages. Many of our men of speculation, instead of exploding general prejudices, employ their sagacity to discover the latent wisdom which prevails in them. If they find what they seek, and they seldom fail, they think it more wise to continue the prejudice, with the reason involved, than to cast away the coat of prejudice, and to leave nothing but the naked reason; because prejudice, with its reason, has a motive to give action to that reason, and an affection which will give it permanence. Prejudice is of ready application in the emergency; it previously engages the mind in a steady course of wisdom and virtue, and does not leave the man hesitating in the moment of decision, sceptical, puzzled, and unresolved. Prejudice renders a man's virtue his habit; and not a series of unconnected acts. Through just prejudice, his duty becomes a part of his nature.[6]

If Burke's approach was to take existing institutions and argue that they had a reason, the approach of Hume and Smith was to start at the other end. They took some very limited assumptions about human nature and showed how these made man fit for society. Adam Smith praised David Hume for observing how:

commerce and manufactures gradually introduced order and good government, and with them, the liberty and security of individuals, among the inhabitants of the country, who had before lived almost in a continual state of war with their neighbours and of servile dependency upon their superiors.[7]

Hume addresses these questions above all in Book III of his *Treatise of Human Nature* where he shows how, paradoxically, the pursuit of self-interest generates co-operation and community.

One argument was that capitalism was of itself a mechanism for enabling us to co-operate with others. As argued in Chapter VI, it was not a device for exploiting others, but a mechanism whereby a host of individual projects came together for mutual benefit. The fundamental instinct to truck, barter and exchange thus leads to spontaneous order.

The other great human institutions – property rights and government – are mechanisms to enable us to enjoy the fruits of our commerce and live in families without being in a perpetual state of anxiety and vulnerability. Those institutions exist to serve human purposes. Hume was at pains to show that this was not a unique British blessing resulting from some special social contract. The French, even the Turks, received similar benefits from their governments. Indeed, all government survived because men appreciated the benefits which they enjoyed from it. The crucial feature of this argument is that man's participation in a community does not rest on some special appeal to Divine authority or to universal benevolence. Instead, it is traced back to a steady and robust understanding of what is in our own interest. These insights have been expressed in the language of modern game theory by Robert Axelrod.[8] He shows that co-operation will emerge even among self-interested individuals provided that they are in a social setting where they have to deal with others repeatedly.

Mobility, Conformity and the Invention of Tradition

The critics reply that this eighteenth-century world, in which social institutions generate harmony out of each individual's pursuit of his own interest, is too neat and cosy. Maybe to the thinkers of the eighteenth century all institutions appeared equally benign and all historical change equally welcome. But the French Revolution forces one to choose between the progressives with a radical agenda of institutional reform, and those who want to conserve what already exists.

The critics also argue that the rapid industrialization of the nineteenth century forces us to face the challenge of rootless, mobile, industrial man. Instead of individuals living in stable communities surrounded by institutions which have grown up over centuries, rapid economic change brought rapid social change. Agricultural communities broke down with massive population shifts to towns, which emerged out of virtually nothing during the century. Manchester grew from 135,000 in 1821 to 502,000 people in 1881, and Birmingham from 102,000 to 546,000 over the same period. This period also experienced a further fracturing of the Anglican community with the emergence of Methodism in the new industrial centres.

What is the conservative response to these changes? One is essentially romantic – to look back to a past when we all knew our place in a pre-industrial community. That gives the elegiac tone to some conservative writing of the past hundred and fifty years. It is emotionally powerful, but it simply fails to address the experience of increasing numbers of British people. The sturdier response is to see how the instinct for community survives, albeit modified, in free industrialized societies. There are perhaps different types of community; that is very different from the disappearance of community. Ease of transport, for example, means that our networks of friends are more dispersed and less limited by immediate neighbourhoods. Similarly, the ties to the land of the stable agricultural economy are weakened and instead we have the experience of working with colleagues in a business.

Our capacity to create these new types of society and rapidly give them a sense of tradition and depth is extraordinary. Within a generation the new industrial towns had established the social conventions and stability of an ancient village. In her book *My Apprenticeship*, Beatrice Webb describes her first piece of social research when she visits the Lancashire mill-town of Bacup in the improbable disguise of Miss Jones, a Welsh farmer's daughter. In the England of the third quarter of the nineteenth century, in a mill-town which had barely existed fifty years previously, she finds a rich communal life with networks of mutual assistance, and poses a question:

How had this class, without administrative training or literary culture, managed to initiate and maintain the network of Non-conformist chapels, the far-flung friendly societies, the much-abused trade unions, and that queer type of shop, the Co-operative Store?[9]

Part of the explanation is to be found in her observation that:

> Certainly the earnest successful working man is essentially conservative as regards the rights of property and the non-interference of the central government . . .[10]

She also shows the importance of the close-knit community in rewarding good behaviour and punishing the bad:

> Public opinion – which means religiously guided opinion – presses heavily on the misdoer or the non-worker – the outcasting process, the reverse of the attracting force of East End life, is seen clearly in this small community, ridding it of the ne'er-do-weel and the habitual out-o'-work. There are no attractions for those who have not sources of love and interest within them; no work for those who cannot or will not work constantly.[11]

All this happened at the peak of free-trade doctrine, with extremely limited government, no welfare state, and massive economic and social change.

Those romantic Tories looking back at ancient traditions too often overlook our remarkable fertility in creating new ones. Part of our capacity to sustain – or, indeed, to create – communities comes from our skill in giving an historical patina to really quite new institutions. The Victorians were brilliant at creating traditions and thus investing the newfangled with historical legitimacy. Richard Shannon observes at the beginning of *The Crisis of Imperialism*: 'The quip that all the oldest English traditions were invented in the last quarter of the nineteenth century has great point.'[12] It is an enjoyable historical game to identify some 'ancient' British institution and trace it back to its supposedly distant origins. Scottish clan tartans (popularized in the mid-nineteenth century); the Festival of Nine Carols and Lessons from King's College Chapel (1918); regular, structured oral parliamentary questions to ministers (1900); the investiture of the Prince of Wales (1911, having lapsed by the seventeenth century). The process of creating a new set of ties to a new place goes on much more rapidly – and we seem to be much more fertile at doing this – than the pessimists allow for. Indeed, some historians claim that 'Englishness' is an invention of the latter half of the nineteenth century.[13]

What can a conservative learn from this? One lesson is that communities and the values which sustain them can be generated remarkably easily in an apparently inhospitable environment. They are a case study in the theories of Smith and Hume.

The Social Market

The Germans formulated their own term, aimed at expressing the mutual dependence between the free market and the community: 'the social market'. It was brought into the British political debate by Keith Joseph in the 1970s. David Owen flirted with it in the 1980s, and it has been given a new lease of life by Chris Patten in the 1990s. Its intellectual origins show that it is not just some woolly expression of a commitment to the mixed economy.

It was originally formulated by the German economic liberals of the Freiburg school. They opposed the cartels, cross-holding of shares, and concentrations of banking power which culminated in Hitler's corporatist control of industry. They argued that Germany needed a powerful anti-cartel policy – the equivalent of American trust-busting – which would ensure that the market fulfilled its social objective of serving consumers. Corporatism had instead created a dangerous military-industrial complex which had served the Nazis. When the German Christian Democrats were reconstituted after World War Two, they embraced this philosophy. The very first of the fundamental Düsseldorf principles, set out by the Christian Democrats in 1949, was: 'Competition, guaranteed by control of monopoly'. They wanted to encourage small and medium-sized businesses. That break-up of the old cartels was crucial to the dramatic growth of the German economy during the 1950s. Underneath all this was a belief that the government's rôle was to ensure open competition. A social market was one addressing the needs of consumers, rather than being subject to political control. It was competition which made markets fulfil their social purpose.

There are further specific economic doctrines behind the idea of a social market; the thought that the government does have a duty not just to ensure genuine competition, but also to maintain stable prices – as otherwise it is much more difficult for markets to function. The rôle of the German Bundesbank in maintaining the integrity of the German currency is now as emotionally significant to the Germans as the rôle of the Académie Française is for the French in maintaining the integrity of their language.

There is also a distinct understanding of the rôle of the firm. Just as the anti-cartel policy involved an appreciation that the firm was not simply something for owners to do with as they wished, so it was also understood that employees had certain rights and that it was in the long-term interests of capitalism itself that these be recognized. This is very much the ethos of the old family firm in Britain, sadly weakened in the postwar period by death duties. The country which has taken this ethos to its furthest extreme is Japan, where firms have their own company god to be worshipped by the workers.

The large modern firm is directly relevant to the theme of this chapter. Advanced Western capitalism is not just a matter for individualistic entrepreneurs (though they are, of course, often the heroes who embody crucial capitalist qualities). The experience of working in a large firm, even if the ultimate corporate objective of that firm is to maximize profits, is not one in which you are on your own, in ruthless pursuit of the profit motive. You are working in a team. The only way your company can survive and flourish is by creating a co-operative spirit in its workforce. By and large, in the process of free competition, it seems to be the case that firms which are most successful in creating a co-operative spirit amongst their workforce flourish and grow at the expense of firms which only see their workers as simple pieces of human capital. Sophisticated capitalism is a highly co-operative experience. We have been so preoccupied with looking at competition between different firms that we have largely overlooked the experience of co-operation within the firm.

This company spirit is a striking contrast with the experience of the former communist regimes. A Western businessman told the author of a visit made to his factory in Britain by company managers from the old East Germany. One thing above all had amazed them – that his employees worked without direct and constant supervision. They said that a factory line in the East, by contrast, would have required foremen walking up and down between the workbenches to check that the men were not shirking. If there was anywhere which was a case study in Marxist alienation from one's work, it was, ironically, the old communist economies. It is not only bad, it is also inefficient to tie up so many men in supervising others – the industrial equivalent of tying up a significant proportion of your educated classes working as secret policemen. Firms operating in a capitalist environment are much more 'social' than those in the old planned economies.

Many people in Germany and Britain think that the social market simply means the capitalist economy with a welfare state. That is certainly also part of the concept – some sort of welfare state and a successful market economy go together. Only a successful, free-enterprise economy can finance a welfare state. Equally, and this is sometimes overlooked, a properly functioning welfare state can make it easier to operate a market economy (an issue discussed further in Chapter X). But even here the term should not be allowed to mislead. It is wrong to assume that the social element must mean state action and public spending. The social market derives not just from Germany's economic liberal tradition, but also from Catholic christian democracy. This recognizes the importance of the 'mediating structures' between the individual and the state. This was encouraged by the Allies after World War Two, who, rightly, understood that a vigorous civil society in Germany would be a bastion against dictatorship. The result is that Germany now has a legal framework setting out the responsibilities of communities such as the family or the firm which is more elaborate than anywhere else in the world. A sophisticated German family law lays down legal obligations between parents and children, for example, which go way beyond what the conventional wisdom would find acceptable here. Industry-wide or locally based contributory insurance funds pay for health care. There is a big rôle for local chambers of commerce in training. The social market is in fact the most sophisticated attempt at defining in economic theory and constitutional law the relationships between the different types of community which comprise the modern nation-state, the operation of the free market, and the government itself.

The social market is now a fundamental part of the political culture of Germany. It is a shared consensus across all political parties; yet fifty years ago it was restricted to discussions amongst free-market German economists in exile in Istanbul. It is an extraordinary example of the capacity to create a new ethos for a country.

Macro- and Micro-conservatism

Two different strands of conservatism were disentangled in Chapter V: the belief in 'the community' and the belief in 'communities'. Nobody has to face the dilemma in quite as vivid a form as this, but it does suggest some theoretical tensions.

On the one hand there is the tradition of Burke – the conservative community of the nation-state – carried forward into the nineteenth century by romantic nationalism. This is what one might call 'macro-conservatism', with a particular set of values embodied in the over-arching national community.

The alternative is what one might call 'micro-conservatism' which emphasizes the particular network of communities which gives each individual life its meaning – from the family and the firm to the neighbourhood, and to friends or relatives or colleagues who may come from another country. The nation-state has a rôle, but a much more modest one, in sustaining a political order in which this multiplicity of communities can thrive. The nation-state can command our loyalty as the protector of these communities but we certainly cannot look to it as one organic whole embodying detailed moral purposes which we all share. If we look at what we love and gives our lives meaning, we find that the nation-state is but one among many.

Markets may make it more difficult to sustain that macro-conservatism and easier to sustain the micro-conservatism of the particular communities. And one of the powerful forces behind this is mobility. Having power to move away from institutions enables people within that institution or within that community to demand higher standards of conformity. They do not have to tolerate diversity of behaviour from people within the neighbourhood, within the firm. If you do not like this sort of rule, they say, you can move somewhere else. Individual communities can be more intense and demand more of their members if the demands of the national political culture are much looser. Take, for example, the debate about whether the Anglican Church should offer the rites of passage – baptism, marriage and funerals – to all British citizens who want them or only to practising Christians. If it is the national Church, embodying a national culture, then it cannot turn people away but, at the same time, its religious practices lose some of their intensity because they will mean little to some of the people engaged in them. It can regain greater religious significance for those rites but only at the cost of abandoning its position as a national institution and settling instead for, say, a status of one particular religious community amongst others.

Perhaps the most vivid example of this is America, which is both highly diverse at the federal level, and also remarkably homogenous at local level. The USA, the world's greatest capitalist country, is also remarkably conformist. In schools, churches, firms and neighbourhoods, Americans gather together with people like themselves. Why is it that the Amish folk have survived in America, when they have not survived on the continent of Europe? The only reason you can have the Amish folk preserving a distinctive community, which is extremely old-fashioned in its values, is because government is so limited. They could not survive in a modern European social democracy. America is not a melting pot but a patchwork quilt – a host of intense and conformist communities.

As the population of advanced Western countries like Great Britain stabilizes, so internal migration becomes the crucial factor changing the character of communities. And one of the powerful forces driving this is simply the desire to live close to people like ourselves. We are moving out from the large, anonymous cities into the countryside or small towns which are much more likely to be fairly homogenous in social terms. The political scientists have picked this up, observing a decline in the number of marginal constituencies because parliamentary constituencies in the United Kingdom are now much less mixed than they were twenty-five years ago. Thus the market brings mobility, and mobility in turn brings a more tightly knit neighbourhood. Indeed, mobility between different neighbourhoods, different types of communities, is itself an important sort of social choice. It means that some communities thrive and others wither in accordance with human preferences, but not driven by any individual's plan.[14]

The Reality of Conservative Capitalism

Reading ingenious theories showing why capitalism cannot survive, one is left wondering why the world seems ever more free-market. The theories of the pessimists who feared the decay of capitalism are out of touch with reality. Capitalism is a more powerful, political and economic movement now than at any other time this century. The advanced Western world remains resolutely committed to Smith's 'system of natural liberty'. The old Eastern bloc and the impoverished third world have not only abandoned Lenin and Che Guevara, but also Dubček and Tito. Adam Smith, Friedrich Hayek, Margaret Thatcher convey the spirit of the age.

Conservative capitalism must have more effective mechanisms to protect itself against the erosion of its moral capital than the pessimists allow for. Our review of postwar conservatism in Chapters III and IV suggested what some of these mechanisms might be. Free-market economies generate growth and prosperity which are nowadays so important in sustaining any democratic polity. Detailed government intervention in the economy fails to deliver the economic growth which modern electorates expect. More fundamentally, it sets us in direct competition with each other for government favours and subsidies. A government which steers clear of heavy-handed intervention eases the pressures of overload and ungovernability which we saw in Britain in the 1970s. And even if we are all tempted to indulge our appetites and to borrow rather than to save (as happened in Britain in the late 1980s) we are soon brought to face the unpalatable reality – that you cannot carry on borrowing to live beyond your means for ever. Painful lessons in prudent borrowing and lending are re-learned.

If one turns to normal people's everyday experience, those fears about the destructive forces unloosed by free markets seem absurd and hysterical. The British suburb is not a place of rootless, miserable apathy. People, admittedly, do pursue their material aspirations – to own their house, to pay off the mortgage, to be able to afford a good holiday – but these are not immoral or shameful. And at the same time the latest sociological researchers confirm what one may anyway have suspected: that suburbs comprise rich networks of voluntary association, from Rotary Club to British Legion, from the rota for driving the children to school to the firm's social club. Even that urge to home ownership, satisfied more successfully in the 1980s than in any other decade, has given people new and stronger ties to their neighbourhood. Ownership and belonging go together. Our civic culture is under greatest strain not in the suburbs but in the inner cities from where so many businesses have fled. It is the absence of a modern capitalist economy which brings the real problems, not its success.

So conservatives can happily value both the historic traditions of this country and the values of freedom and the free market. There is no need to become bogged down in arguments about which of these ideas should take precedence – because we have the good fortune to live in a society which has a long historical tradition of freedom and individualism.

CHAPTER VIII:

Socialism and Equality

Conservatism rests on a deep understanding of the sources of human satisfaction. It brings together the crucial values of freedom and the need for community in a coherent and attractive way. And it speaks to people at the end of the twentieth century as powerfully as at any time in our history. But there is one key idea, seductive, and with a strong emotional appeal, which cannot be absorbed into conservative thought: egalitarianism. Socialism may be dying but not the idea of equality. It is now the key, anti-conservative concept. It stands out all the more clearly as the detritus of socialism surrounding it is cleared away.

There are three different strands to socialist thought: the Marxist, the Fabian and the egalitarian. Marxism claims to have a scientific account of the course of human history in which the internal contradictions of capitalism, in particular the tendency for ever-increasing numbers of workers to become ever poorer, eventually leads to revolutionary transformation into communism. Insofar as any such theory can be open to refutation, it has been. Its intellectual collapse deprived communist regimes of any legitimacy and they too have collapsed. The death of Marxism has long been obvious in the 'harder' disciplines such as economics. As it decays, so its followers retreat into subjects such as art criticism or literary theory – an ironic fate given its claims to be a science. Like light from a long-dead star which is still reaching the further ends of the galaxy, so Marxism may carry on spreading into such disciplines long after it is intellectually dead. Doubtless a theatre director who believes he is being *avant garde* will try to shock us with a Marxist interpretation of *The Pirates of Penzance* in about 1997. But none of this will disguise the fact that Marxism is extinct.

The Fabian belief in the superiority of the state over the market was discussed in Chapter II. Followers of the Fabians believe the market is unplanned, irrational, haphazard – whereas detailed direction of economic activity by the state in a command economy is supposed to yield rationality, justice and progress. That was one of the most vigorous intellectual movements earlier in the century. It has laid waste great countries such as India and what were some of our more prosperous African colonies. It is now in retreat.

What remains is the third element in socialist thought: the commitment to equality. The two great British socialist tracts of this century (Tawney's *Equality* of 1931 and Crosland's *Future of Socialism* of 1956) both argue for egalitarianism as the core of socialism. Whereas the works of Marx and of the socialist statists are not only obviously wrong but also chillingly unpleasant, the same cannot be said of these egalitarian texts. They appeal to noble sentiments:

> What is repulsive is not that one man should earn more than others ... it is that some classes should be excluded from the heritage of civilisation which others enjoy, and that the face of human fellowship, which is ultimate and profound, should be obscured by economic contrasts which are trivial and super-ficial.[1]

Egalitarianism goes back long before socialism and will long outlast it.

Tawney's egalitarian argument is one which any conservative can understand because it rests on an appeal to our sense of community. If a conservative community is one in which we share a history, culture, values and unspoken assumptions, why should we not also all share equally in the nation's wealth and income? Why should the distribution of income and wealth be dependent on the operation of the market rather than reflect the values of the community?

Different Sorts of Equality

There are certain sorts of equality which every modern conservative must accept as the rights of any Briton. We are, for moral and constitutional purposes, all egalitarians now. The duke and the dustman are of equal moral worth. We all have equal political rights. We all accept Colonel Rainborough's famous statement in the Putney debates after the English Civil War: 'The poorest he that is in England hath a life to live, as the greatest he.' We all expect equal treatment before the law. These are part of the political culture of this country and constitute 'procedural justice'. There are no groups enjoying something like diplomatic immunity for whom the normal laws do not apply. (The closest we come to that is still the legal immunity which trade unions enjoy from normal legal liability for damages they cause.) The modern British constitution does ensure procedural justice, and that itself is an important sort of equality.

At the other end of the scale are the fundamental inequalities of the natural order: inequalities in looks, in intelligence, in talents and prudence. We are not equally good singers or runners. We have different aptitudes. Egalitarianism can easily be mocked by imagining (as, for example, L. P. Hartley does in *Facial Justice*) that we should all be made equally good-looking.

The intellectual battleground between conservatives and socialists is over economic inequality – differences in income and wealth. For the socialists, if we all have equal moral status, and equal voting rights, our incomes and wealth should also be broadly equal. They are seen as part of the political arrangements of a country (just like voting rights) and should be decided upon explicitly and politically settled. For the conservative, economic equalities are much more like parts of the natural order which are – or ought to be – outside explicit political decision. We tamper with them at our peril. There is a clear dividing line between the market allocation of resources, and fundamental constitutional rights. As Burke put it: 'All men have equal rights; but not to equal things.'[2]

The modern democratic order defines the areas – voting, juries, legal process – where we do not allow markets to decide. Jurors do not auction their decision on whether somebody is guilty or not. Keeping the political and the commercial apart is a great achievement. Just as we do not want commerce to corrupt political rights, so we do not want politics to corrupt economic transactions.

Sometimes egalitarians try to muddle up this clear question by talking about 'social justice'. What they are trying to do with this slippery term is to imply that equal command over resources is somehow the same as procedural justice on which we are all egalitarian. But the only clear and consistent meaning one can give to the rhetoric of social justice is the pursuit of ever-greater material equality. That is the issue.

The Egalitarian Muddle

The emotional appeal of the idea of equality is only matched by its vagueness. A serious socialist has to be committed to trying to equalize incomes and wealth. Perhaps the most rigorous and moderate recent statement of the egalitarian position is in Rawls' *Theory of Justice* in which he argues that:

> All social primary goods – liberty and opportunity, income and wealth, and the bases of self-respect – are to be distributed equally unless an unequal distribution of any or all of these goods is to the advantage of the least favoured.[3]

There is one way of reconciling Rawls with conservative wariness of egalitarianism. Rawls has the crucial get-out clause that inequalities are to be tolerated if they benefit the poorest members of society. There are perfectly respectable economic arguments that a society with a wide distribution of income and wealth enjoys greater prosperity in which even the poorest members of that society share. The economic and social policy of Conservative governments since 1979 can be defended along these lines. If you have a wide set of wage differentials then there are greater incentives for people to improve their skills – and the performance of industry improves. Rich private individuals will invest in a much greater variety of activities that either a politician or an institution. And, of course, as was argued in Chapter VI, free markets are not a zero-sum game; his being rich is not the reason you are poor.

But simply to rest the case against egalitarianism on these practical points would be to concede too much. Egalitarianism is not just wrong in practice; it is also wrong in principle. And this is where the real argument begins. Many people accept that you could not really operate egalitarian policies in practice, because, tiresomely, all the rich people would take their money to some tax haven. But at the same time they believe that a morally upright world would be egalitarian. They only accept inequality as a sadly necessary lapse from a high ideal.

The appeal of egalitarianism is that it seems to combine the principle of fairness with extreme simplicity; it cuts through the elaborate arguments about what is fair by the straightforward application of a mathematical rule. It is the logic of a mother with one cake and four argumentative children dividing it up into equal quarters. It is the obvious thing to do. It requires no justification, whereas any other division of the cake does.[4]

The first objection to the principle is that as soon as we try to move equality from the realms of mathematics to the realms of real societies, we discover that equality is not so simple after all. Indeed, it is deeply muddled. It is equality between who, in respect of what, and when? A few simple examples will show the difficulties. Michael Novack (author of *The Spirit of Democratic Capitalism*) cites the case of two unmarried sisters each inheriting £50,000. One spends the money on good foreign holidays and trips to the theatre, so that after ten years it is all gone. The other invests shrewdly, so that after ten years it has doubled. Each has got genuine satisfaction from their own behaviour. Neither envies the other. In fact, each regards her sister as misguided and her behaviour as rather bizarre. At what point, if any, are we supposed to step in and equalize their position? Are they equal after ten years? Would it be fair to take the £100,000 accumulated by one sister, divide it between them and start all over again? As soon as one ceases to respect their right to do what they wish with their own money, and puts oneself in the position of some arch-distributor, it becomes clear that there is no straightforward moral approach to be taken.

The slow process whereby we accumulate property further complicates the idea of equality. Most of us are born property-less, but on average a pensioner has net assets that are 50 per cent higher than those of a non-pensioner. (The statistics supposedly showing great disparities of income and wealth in advanced Western countries are much less striking when adjusted for such simple effects of the life cycle.) Again, what is a 'fair' redistribution policy? Are we to redistribute across the ages, from old to young? Is it unfair that the average sixty-year-old owns more than the average twenty-year-old, or is this an acceptable pattern of economic life?

And within a similar age group, consider the university student managing on a modest grant and loan as against a contemporary who works on the shopfloor and has a much higher income. If you have been a student you are likely to have been, statistically speaking, very poor indeed. But we know that the lifetime earnings of the student are likely to be much higher than the earnings of the shopfloor worker without a university qualification. Should we redistribute between them now? And if so, in what direction? Or how about a single man earning £15,000 a year and a married man earning £20,000 a year with a non-working wife and two young children? Who is earning more? What if we ask instead: 'Who is more prosperous?' How would we equalize their incomes?

These practical examples show why the image of the mother dividing the cake between her four children is so misleading, because then we could assume there were no relevant differences between the four. As children they have not had to take important decisions about the pattern of their lives. And the mother has a control over them most of us would never dream of giving to the state. Out there, in the wider world, differences in income arise from reasonable choices we can make about how we live our lives. They are not the result of some evil, social or economic conspiracy. Our choices may be constrained by circumstances, and for some people those constraints may be more serious than for others; nevertheless, in an open society we do all have scope to make those choices. The incomes and property which result from them do, indeed, rightly belong to us.

Saying our property is our property may sound rather unadventurous. But it is directly challenged by Rawls's argument that we need to justify any difference in income and wealth and that it will only be tolerated if it is shown to raise the living standards of the least well-off members of society. Why should we be obliged to defend our property in those terms when it is so tied up with our life choices and our decisions about how we wish to live? It is as if someone challenged a married couple to show each morning why they should not be divorced. The whole assumption behind the language of 'redistribution' is that somehow there was some previous explicit single 'distribution' which is open to question. But there was no such conscious distribution, merely a pattern of income and wealth that emerged from a host of personal and sometimes unplanned decisions. The onus is on the egalitarians to show why they wish to use the coercive power of the state to interfere with that.

There are legitimate grounds for resources to be taken from some to be used for wider social purposes. But the question for the egalitarian is whether equality in itself is one of those grounds. After all, what is so special about simply equalizing incomes? We can understand liberty as a powerful political principle. Fraternity is also an attractive concept. Both are political, indeed moral, ideas. But equality is just arithmetic. Why should it have any political relevance? The challenge to justify inequality can be turned round and thrown back at the egalitarians: what is so special about equality; how do they justify massive state interference in incomes and wealth so as to equalize them? Some egalitarians have responded to that challenge by conceding that they are no longer interested in equality for its own sake. Instead, equality is justified as the means to some higher political goal – greater liberty or greater fraternity. It is to these arguments that I now turn.

Equality, Liberty and Opportunity

It is not always easy to attach precise meanings to words used in everyday political argument. Nevertheless the attempt by some revisionist socialists, such as Roy Hattersley, to mix up the ideas of equality and freedom seems just to be a deliberate attempt to confuse the issue. Like an octopus under attack, they squirt out their ink in an attempt to confuse us all. The argument seems to go like this: freedom really means practical opportunities to shape and control one's own life; socialist egalitarianism means spreading these practical opportunities as widely as possible; egalitarianism therefore means maximizing freedom.

The usual conservative response is to criticize the first stage of this slippery argument. There is a crucial distinction between 'freedom from' and 'freedom to'. The first sense is a strict and precise meaning of freedom as the absence of coercion. The second, broader interpretation gives freedom a meaning which is close to 'opportunity' or 'power'. Conservatives say it is best to stick to the strict meaning of freedom. Despite what the revisionist egalitarians may believe, it does make sense to say that someone is both poor and free – that means they live in a society governed by the rule of the law in which they can freely express their opinions and freely vote. Nobody is banning us from having lunch at the Ritz; we are free to do so; it is just that we cannot afford it.

This classic argument does, however, leave one with a feeling of unease. That narrow definition of freedom may well be clear, correct and useful. But it does not follow that the other idea – having opportunities to control and shape one's own life – is unimportant. Indeed, the rhetorical power of appeals to freedom in many a Conservative speech rests on a much broader sense of it than the limited one which the purists are prepared to accept. If council house sales have not increased people's freedom in the strict sense of the term, they have nevertheless still given millions of people a greater sense of controlling their own lives. If we have to call this opportunity, rather than freedom, we might think that in that case opportunity matters almost as much as freedom. And if the socialists could successfully show that egalitarian policies on income and wealth did indeed spread opportunities, then it would be a significant point in their favour, even if we did not call it freedom.

Setting aside all the wordplay, therefore, the important question out in the real world is whether it is socialism or capitalism which best opens up opportunities for people to control their own lives. The answer is clear. Its classic exposition is in de Tocqueville's *Democracy in America*. He first saw in America a model of a modern, democratic society which would open opportunities for its citizens and spread them more widely than any other conceivable social arrangement. Indeed, this opening up of opportunities is in a sense egalitarian. It is what would now be called 'equality of opportunity'. Here is de Tocqueville's account of it:

> The value attached to the privileges of birth decreased in the exact proportion in which new paths were struck out to advancement . . . as soon as land was held on any than a feudal tenure, and personal property began in its turn to counter influence and power, every improvement which was introduced in commerce or manufacture was a fresh element of the equality of conditions . . . the divisions which once severed mankind are lowered; property is divided, power is held in common, the light of intelligence spreads, and the capacities of all classes are equally cultivated; the State becomes democratic and the empire of democracy is slowly and peaceably introduced into the institutions and manners of the nation.[5]

This so-called 'capitalist equality', or 'equality of opportunity', differs from the socialist pursuit of egalitarianism in two crucial respects. First of all, the free-market system, which so powerfully spreads these opportunities, needs disparities of income and wealth in order to function. You cannot have free markets without price signals. It is through higher wages that the market signals that talents or skills are in short supply and training is worthwhile. It is the prospect of acquiring wealth to pass on to one's family which motivates many entrepreneurs. This is how a society with freedom of opportunity works.

Secondly, the state's rôle is limited. The project of equalizing income and wealth requires an enormous concentration of power in the hands of the state. That centralization of power would itself be a terrible threat to democratic civil societies. Such an overarching state perpetually redistributing income would also undermine people's control over their own lives. Most of the normal routes to independence – improving one's income or saving some money – would be taken away. That represents an enormous loss of opportunities to control one's own life.

Equality, Fraternity and the Welfare State

Egalitarians who recognize that equality cannot stand on its own feet sometimes link it not to freedom but to fraternity. They argue that if we are all to enjoy a proper sense of solidarity and engagement with our fellow citizens, then we need genuine economic equality. Anything less makes the conservative vision of community bogus, they argue.

One can certainly concede that in a modern free-market economy it is difficult to see how someone can participate properly without some command over resources. One of the reasons why we are prepared, through our taxes, to pay for social security is to ensure that people with no other source of income have an adequate standard of living. It could be called a gesture of fraternity towards our fellow citizens. But that falls far short of the equality which socialists press on us.

Moreover, as soon as one has passed these basic income requirements, it is clear that participation in the life of the community is by no means a simple economic matter. It is much more important that someone has some sense of their country's history and culture. However large the girocheque may be, if the person receiving it has had such a bad education that they do not know who Winston Churchill was, and have never come into contact with the writing of Charles Dickens, then they are indeed at risk of being disinherited from their own community. And it is a sad irony that those on the left who are so keen on arguing that money brings participation have encouraged fashionable educational theories in some of our state schools which are a much greater threat to people's participation in their own society.

Some argue that the welfare state rests on egalitarian principles and therefore if one does not believe in equality, one must oppose the welfare state. But as Chapter X will show, there are perfectly good conservative arguments for publicly financed education, health care and a social security system which have nothing to do with equality. Sir William Beveridge called us all, in marvellously Bunyanesque words, to attack Want, Disease, Ignorance, Squalor and Idleness. Those are battles worth fighting in their own right, without being distracted by the will-o'-the-wisp of egalitarianism.

PART III:

POLICIES

CHAPTER IX:

Economic Policy

Modern democratic politics is about economics. The most important single factor determining the outcome of elections is voters' optimism about their personal economic prospects. Some high-minded nineteenth-century reformers believed that extending the franchise would raise the tone of elections. Instead of the corruption of pocket boroughs, there would be argument about high moral issues on which everyone had an equal right to form their own judgement. But even if Gladstone was able to fight and win the 1880 election on the issue of the Bulgarian massacres, Lloyd George's slogan for his new national insurance scheme in the 1910 general election – Ninepence for Fourpence – set the standard for modern campaigns.

This link between politics and economics may be regarded by some Tories as a consequence of what they see as the regrettable vulgarity of the populace. That is too shallow a judgement. A nation's economic performance is closely related to its whole political culture. The problem of inflation in postwar Britain is a classic example of the link between economics and deeper social problems. We are all familiar with the truism that inflation is too much money chasing too few goods. It arises when the spending plans of a nation's citizens exceed their productive capacity. (The only alternative to inflation in such circumstances is to run a balance of payments deficit, and that is unlikely to be sustainable over the long term.) Inflation reduces the real value of these spending plans and thus ensures that they match the actual output of the economy.

Inflation carries out a necessary social function in a disordered society in which people's appetites exceed their capacities. To do this, its erosion of people's spending plans has to be unanticipated – people do not get what they expect. If inflation were perfectly anticipated, and every contract fully and frequently indexed so that they all represented absolutely fixed claims on real resources, then inflation could not do its grim job. This is one of the reasons why it tends to accelerate – if we are all used to 5 per cent inflation, an increase to 10 per cent is needed in order to make us unexpectedly poorer; and as we get used to that, so we need 20 per cent inflation to do the same job.

Inflation is not just evidence that people are dissatisfied with their lot: it also, in turn, contributes to that dissatisfaction – it cuts back our spending plans by eroding the real value of our incomes during the year. A worker with an annual wage settlement in an economy with 15 per cent inflation suffers a large drop in living standards over the year. He has an average income $7\frac{1}{2}$ per cent lower than he was promised at the beginning of the year. By the time the following year's pay negotiations begin, he has had to cope with a 15 per cent fall in his real income. If any one single factor drove industrial militancy during the 1970s, it was this 'eleventh hour effect' of inflation on people's income: big falls in their living standards during the year left them feeling angry, betrayed and disheartened. That is very dangerous for any country's political stability.

Inflation is not therefore a narrow, economic problem to be solved exclusively by technocrats whilst the serious business of politics is elsewhere. A society experiencing inflation is one in which people are not reconciled to the actual capacity of their own economy. It is the modern equivalent of an ancient monarchy with territorial ambitions beyond its military capacity. Whatever the immediate technical remedies in financial policy, the underlying solution must be political – in the short run, to lower people's material expectations (roughly the approach of the early 1980s), and in the longer run, to raise the growth rate of the economy so that it can match their increasing appetites (the achievement of the mid and late 1980s).

Success in economic management is the most important single measure of the effectiveness and coherence of a party's political programme. Of course any serious political vision must look far beyond economic management. But success in one's economic policies is the best and clearest piece of evidence that the electorate can use to judge whether a party's programme rests on a sure foundation.

Monetarism

'Monetarism' hovers over accounts of economic policy in the 1980s like a poltergeist in a horror film. For many commentators it is at best mumbo-jumbo[1] or at worst, the wilful mistreatment of the British economy (Denis Healey called it 'sado-monetarism'). Indeed, its connotations are now so politically unpalatable that Conservatives have, by and large, stopped using the word. This is a pity because monetarism, properly understood, remains the only sound basis for economic policy. It can safely be summarized in three propositions which constitute the core of Conservative economics since 1979.

The first proposition is that inflation is a monetary phenomenon. It is caused by governments running too loose a financial policy, thus allowing the total amount of money circulating in the economy to increase by more than real output can grow. The gap is inflation. (The political account of inflation offered above was an explanation of the social background which creates a need for inflation: this is an account of how governments respond to that need.) This monetarist account of inflation can be traced back in economic thought long before Professor Milton Friedman; it is to be found in Keynes's own *Treatise on Money*. Perhaps its most lucid exposition was provided by David Hume writing in 1752:

> ... though the high price of commodities be a necessary consequence of the increase of gold and silver, yet it follows not immediately upon that increase; but some time is required before the money circulates through the whole State, and it makes its effects be felt on all ranks of people. At first, no alteration is perceived; by degrees the price rises first of one commodity, then of another, then of another; 'til the whole at last reaches a just proportion with the new quantity of specie which is in the kingdom. In my opinion, it is only in this interval or intermediate situation, between the acquisition of money and rise of prices, that the increasing quantity of gold and silver is favourable to industry.[2]

The clue to reconciling monetarism and Keynesianism is to be found in Hume's concession that in the short term, an increase in the money supply is a stimulus to real output. The monetarist emphasizes that this is only temporary. Indeed it only arises at all because inflation in its early stages misleads people into thinking that they are being offered a higher real price for their goods and services, and so they supply more. But these higher prices are eroded by inflation and real levels of output end up back where they were. A Keynesian will point out that the *General Theory* is explicitly an account of the short-term behaviour of an economy and Keynes was not interested in the long-term effects of his policies. He famously observed that 'in the long run, we are all dead'; to which one monetarist replied: 'Now Keynes is dead and we are in the long run'.

The second monetarist proposition is that the rate of growth of money-spending in an economy needs to be limited by some open and explicit financial rule. This is a necessary discipline for policy-makers. It also signals to people and firms that if they push up their prices, that is a real increase which will not be eroded by inflation; as a result, they risk pricing themselves out of work or business.

The argument against having a financial rule is that the government is creating a rod for its own back. With an economy as complicated as ours, and so susceptible to external influences such as the oil price, the pragmatists say it is impossible for the government to follow one financial rule to the exclusion of all others. Financial rectitude is admirable but it can only be sensibly pursued by looking at the evidence from a host of different financial indicators. Moreover, even if one indicator has in the past had a stable and reliable relationship with the ultimate objective of inflation, there is no reason, especially after the government starts trying to target it, why that relationship should carry on being valid. (This is known as Goodhart's Law: when a measure becomes a target it ceases to be a reliable measure.)

The trouble is that looking at all the different financial indicators, taking everything into account, and interpreting the evidence on a pragmatic basis, leaves financial markets, businessmen and pay negotiators completely unsure of where they stand. And if they cannot be sure what the guidelines of policy are, or how the government will react, then the financial markets will always fear the worst – suspecting that the evidence will be interpreted to give the politically convenient conclusion. They will demand a risk premium on the interest rates at which they lend. Wage bargainers do not believe the government is serious and press for big pay increases. If the government then refuses to bail them out with the inflation they expect, then their increases in pay rates will price them out of work, causing unemployment. This is indeed the explanation of why the 1979–81 recession was so deep: the government stuck to its policies but it was untested and nobody believed that it would. Credibility is a very precious asset: it greatly eases the task of economic management. When it comes to financial policy, pragmatism does not work. It would be much better if everyone believed that the Chancellor of the Exchequer and the Governor of the Bank of England were narrow-minded ideologues as obsessed with getting inflation down as Ludwig of Bavaria was with Wagner's operas.

The third monetarist proposition is that the only way to improve the underlying rate of growth of the economy is by measures which liberate the supply side. If Keynesians offer the stimulus of caffeine tablets, supply-siders offer fitness training – deregulation to ease burdens on business, and a better workforce moving freely to jobs where they can generate the greatest wealth. It is essential for the efficiency of any economy that prices be free to change relative to each other, to signal where resources are best being used. If a highly profitable company is expanding fast and needs more workers, it has to be able to increase its pay rates relative to others in the area. If a company is booming and wants to raise more capital, it needs to be able to pay out larger dividends which tempt in more investment.

As was discussed in Chapter III, the original appeal of Keynesianism in the 1930s had been that it apparently offered a way out of the Great Depression without government getting involved in the detailed regulation of the economy which the socialists wanted. It was part of the intellectual decay of

Keynesianism during the 1960s and 1970s that it increasingly came to rely on detailed government controls in the economy, which made it very difficult for markets to operate efficiently. Keynesianism became socialism. By the time that the Conservative government came to power in 1979 it had to remove price controls, dividend controls, not-quite-statutory pay controls, exchange controls, and subsidies to hold down the price of politically sensitive goods such as food.

Nigel Lawson neatly summarized these crucial monetarist propositions and their challenge to the conventional wisdom in his Mais Lecture delivered in 1984:

> The conventional postwar wisdom was that unemployment was a consequence of inadequate economic growth and economic growth was to be secured by *macro*-economic policy – the fiscal stimulus of an enlarged budget deficit, with monetary policy (to the extent that it could be said to exist at all) on the whole passively following fiscal policy. Inflation, by contrast, was increasingly seen as a matter to be dealt with by *micro*-economic policy – the panoply of controls and subsidies associated with the era of incomes policy.
>
> But the proper rôle of each is precisely the opposite of that assigned to it by the conventional postwar wisdom. It is the conquest of inflation, and not the pursuit of growth and employment, which is or should be the objective of macro-economic policy. And it is the creation of conditions conducive to growth and employment, and not the suppression of price rises, which is or should be the objective of micro-economic policy.
>
> The most important point to emphasise is that this government is pursuing simultaneously both a macro and a micro policy, that the one complements the other, that the macro policy is unequivocally directed at the continuing reduction in inflation with the ultimate objective of stable prices, and that the micro policy is equally whole-heartedly designed to make the economy work better and thus generate more jobs.

The Search for the Right Financial Rule

The proposition that there should be some financial rule, discussed above, would probably get the support of most economic policy-makers now. But all through the 1980s the government was dogged by arguments about what that rule should be. It made monetarism seem more controversial than it really was.

In the nineteenth century the rule was the gold standard. Under the Bretton Woods system (1946 to 1971) all other currencies were linked to the dollar, which was in turn linked to gold. The period, 1971–6, when there was no financial rule disciplining the economic policy of the British government, was probably the most disastrous period of economic management in our country's history. The government could run as loose a policy as it liked without having to worry about the foreign exchange markets. It briefly stimulated growth but, as Hume had explained, it soon exhausted the capacity of the economy to grow and inflation was the result.

In 1976, under pressure from the International Monetary Fund (IMF), the then Labour government introduced domestic monetary targets – a new form of financial rule. They were also the core of the Thatcher government's Medium Term Financial Strategy (MTFS), first set out in 1980. The domestic monetary targets took various forms until, in 1990, the government joined the Exchange Rate Mechanism (ERM) of the European Monetary System (EMS) and thus went back to an exchange rate rule for financial policy, though this time linked to the Deutschmark, not the dollar or gold. It was the end of the heroic, fourteen-year period of 'monetarism in one country'.

A lot of the criticism which appeared to be directed against monetarist financial rules per se was merely against the particular domestic monetary rule actually chosen. The very same people who denounced the government for trying to stick to targets of growth for the domestic money supply as an absurd ideological obsession were often advocates of joining the ERM, tying the pound to the Deutschmark and thus to Germany's own domestic monetary targets. Nigel Lawson's first Treasury paper recommending membership of the ERM, submitted to Geoffrey Howe in September 1981, argued that the so-called wets who so opposed domestic monetary targets were also Europhiles and would support exactly the same financial discipline if it were presented in a European context.

Ideally a rule should be so widely accepted as part of a nation's political culture and its assumptions about economic policy, that people don't even realize it could be broken. Modern governments want to take the key which unlocks inflation, tie it to a stone and throw it deep into the ocean, never to use it again. That is the thinking behind the various proposals for new financial rules, or an independent central bank, or a new currency commission. The difficulty in doing this is very similar to the difficulty in genuine nuclear disarmament: the knowledge exists and we cannot return to a prelapsarian world in which nobody has ever thought of devaluing the currency and conducting a loose monetary policy.

If the monetarist policies outlined above make such marvellous sense, why is it that at the beginning of the 1990s the British economy found itself once more in a miserable recession? Why has the economy gone through a roller-coaster of unsustainable boom in the late 1980s, followed by inflation and a balance of payments deficit and then the slide into a recession almost as uncomfortable as 1979–81 and 1974–5? Surely this is old-fashioned stop-go with a vengeance? It is as if the British economy were behaving like an impatient man in a shower – step in and it is too cold; turn it on hot and scald yourself; turn it down again and freeze. Surely monetarism was supposed to stop all that?

It is generally accepted amongst economists that the source of our difficulties lies in the loosening of monetary conditions in the late 1980s. Mrs Thatcher blames the shadowing of the Deutschmark during 1988 at a period when it was weak: an exchange rate rule, instead of being a financial discipline, became a source of laxity. The Treasury looks back a bit further, to the 1987 stock market crash when most of the experts feared that the world would enter a recession just as it did after the 1929 crash; that was why they made the honest mistake of loosening policy too much. The loosening of policy could be traced back as far as 1986. That is when the big fall in sterling took place –

from nearly 4 DM to 3 DM – prompted by the dramatic fall in oil prices that year. At the time this was seen as a sensible devaluation, reflecting the fact that one of Britain's major assets – its North Sea oil – lost nearly half its value. There was also a political element; after the Westland crisis and with unemployment still rising, the government looked in a weak position politically; there was a great temptation to tolerate that weakening of sterling because of the political benefit of a temporary stimulus to the economy. The temptation was all the greater because the government had already lost confidence in sterling M3 (or 'broad' money, which includes bank deposits) as an accurate monetary indicator and the new preferred target of M0, or 'narrow' money (notes and coin together with bankers' deposits at the Bank of England) was not widely respected or properly tested. The original framework of the Medium Term Financial Strategy had been largely abandoned without anything being put in its place. Thus, between the beginning of 1986 and the end of 1988 there was a persistent tendency for the conduct of financial policy to err on the side of laxity. Everything else followed from that.

But this is not the end of the story. There were deeper forces at work making it difficult for the government to maintain a tight monetary policy successfully. Turn away from the financial data to demographic shifts which drive fundamental changes in the economy. The 1980s saw a big increase in the number of people in their twenties, together with increasing numbers of divorcees and single-parent families, and more old people living alone. This added up to an enormous increase in the number of households – well over one million. Together with the planning constraints on building the houses to meet demand, this drove the boom in the housing market. At the same time, the government was deregulating financial services, making it easier for people to borrow, and most borrowing is mortgages. People's borrowing rose in relation to their incomes.

This account of what went wrong shows the mistakes in the conventional criticisms of Conservative economic policy. First of all, tax cuts had very little to do with the excessive stimulus to the economy. Even after excluding receipts from privatizations, the government was running a large budget surplus throughout most of the 1980s. The 1988 tax cuts totalled at most £4 billion, whereas personal borrowing in that year grew by £40 billion. The problem was in monetary policy, not fiscal policy. What we have, therefore, is not a refutation but a tragic vindication of monetarism.

Secondly, we are told that if only we had joined the ERM back in 1985 none of this would have happened. The trouble with this is that of itself, joining the ERM does nothing to tighten policy. The test would have come when oil prices fell during 1986 and the pound came under pressure. Would the government then have devalued in the ERM, or would it have increased interest rates substantially so as to tighten policy with an election looming? It is possible after all to run a sound financial policy outside the ERM; the government did that in its first seven years in office. Provided one has the political will to maintain a tight policy and raise interest rates, the exact form of the financial rule which results is of secondary importance.

But perhaps the most damaging line of criticism is that the mishandling of the economy in the late 1980s has brought Britain back to where she started in 1979: that unemployment, the balance of payments deficit and high inflation show that the economy really faces exactly the same underlying problems as it did then. In particular, the balance of payments deficit of the late 1980s is taken as evidence that the British industrial base is still very weak. But no economy which saw an increase in domestic demand of approximately 15 per cent would be able to meet that by a 15 per cent increase in output. Instead, some of the extra spending would either go on imports or in higher prices. Indeed, the response of the supply side of the British economy in 1987, 1988 and 1989, when it grew by about 5 per cent a year, was extremely good by historic standards. The balance of payments deficit absorbed some of the rest of the pressure. To run a balance of payments deficit with such a stimulus to the economy is not a sign of industrial weakness; it is a sign that financial policy has become too loose.

An economic cycle is inescapable. The important thing is the trend line around which the cycle takes place – and it is clear that that trend is much better than it was ten years ago. Productivity is higher and the underlying growth rate of the British economy is greater than it was in the 1970s. Most European economies grew more slowly during the 1980s than during the 1970s – only the British economy improved during the 1980s on its performance in the 1970s. And having lagged behind continental European countries during the 1970s, we did at least as well as them in the 1980s.

Nevertheless, this supposed failure of the British supply side has led some politicians to urge the old nostrums of corporatism and industrial strategies. It is to these that we now turn.

Corporatism: the Alternative to Monetarism

We are told there is an alternative to all this hard-headed, supply-side, free-market economics. There should be co-operation between trade unions, employers and the government aimed at rebuilding Britain's industrial base. These conventional views have been a staple part of British political discussion since at least World War One. Many British people would think them simple common sense and some, drawing on wartime attitudes, would think of them as morally noble. Many now believe that some of the world's most successful economies operate on precisely these lines. Why, then, does a modern conservative set himself so strongly against these ideas?

There are serious objections of principle to such a corporatist view of politics. Perhaps the most unpleasant term in the political vocabulary is 'UK Limited'. Britain is a country in which people pursue their own purposes, not a firm pursuing a simple commercial objective such as maximizing profits or exports. We cannot all be fitted into a grand economic plan like subsidiaries of a large conglomerate.

But there are other, more down-to-earth, practical reasons. First of all, it is not at all clear that the foreign examples which are so often cited really make the case at all. The rôle of government in German and Japanese industry is much exaggerated. The Ministry of International Trade (MITI) in Tokyo may boast to foreigners of its great rôle in Japan's industrial success, but the domestic reality in Japan is very different. MITI planned to have one Japanese car-maker taking on the world market from a secure, dominant, domestic position. But it could not restrain the entrepreneurial spirit of Japanese industrialists and Japan ended up with at least three major motor car manufacturers. German concerted action between government, employers and unions had been abandoned by the mid-1960s.

The true corporatist economies, with close co-operation between government and industry, are the small, fringe economies of Europe such as Austria and Sweden. There is no denying their postwar prosperity. And it is true that their governments do have a considerable rôle in industry. They are Denis Healey's dream. But they also show that at least three conditions have to be met before government/industry partnership has any chance of working. Firstly there has to be widespread acceptance of an external financial rule which is not part of the negotiations between government and industry. Austria is part of the Deutschmark zone. Sweden, for a long time, maintained a firm exchange rate (and the devaluations of the 1980s are part of the collapse of Swedish corporatism). Secondly, a concentrated industrial structure is needed so that there are a small number of key industrialists all known to each other and to government. It helps indeed if they are family firms linked by inter-marriage, as is the case in Sweden. Finally, trade union leaders need considerable authority over their members so that they can enforce the deals which they negotiate with the government. None of these conditions applied in postwar Britain.

The record of our attempts at government–industry partnership since World War Two is of almost unmitigated disaster. Surveying the evidence, any practical man would conclude that this just does not work in Britain. During the 1950s we spent up to 3 per cent of our entire national output on civil nuclear power and after forty years of government intervention have ended up with an industry which is in a complete muddle and has never exported a single nuclear power station. American commercial aircraft-makers went for wide-bodied jets when sophisticated Whitehall planners decided to back Concorde. Politicians in Whitehall are not there to take decisions according to commercial criteria and it is naïve to expect that they can do a better job than businessmen.

We are told that there is a problem of short-termism and that the government should do more to encourage research and development. But rigorous analysis of the evidence does not support the belief that the City is only interested in short-term profits. What is true about the City is that because share prices already embody all known information about a firm and its economic prospects, then it tends to react rapidly and dramatically to new information: that is the working of an efficient market. It is not short-termism; indeed, it may react to new information in a dramatic but 'long-term' way. If a company announces a big increase in its R & D expenditure, its share price tends to rise rather than to fall.

Actually we do know what leads to long-term improvements in a country's industrial performance. There is no great mystery about it. It has been exhaustively studied in a magisterial survey, by Professor Porter of Harvard University, of industries and companies that are successful. He summarized the argument of his book *The Competitive Advantage of Nations* thus:

> Innovation and upgrading result not from a comfortable home environment in which risks have been minimised, but from pressure and challenge – from demanding home customers, from capable home-based suppliers and most of all from local rivalry. In my research I found that the most internationally competitive industries in every nation were those where there were a number of able local rivals that pressured one another to advance. Examples are American software and consumer packaged goods, German cars and chemicals, Italian fabrics and packaging machinery, and Swedish heavy trucks . . .
>
> Many Americans think Japanese companies have succeeded because of co-operation, cartels, and government intervention. Japan does have many cartels – such as in agriculture, chemicals, construction, paper and metals – but these are in sectors where Japan is not competitive. In the world-class Japanese industries there are numerous Japanese rivals that have diverse strategies. These companies slug it out daily in the home market. Market

shares fluctuate rapidly, as new products and production improvements are introduced at a stunning rate.

Japan's 9 automobile companies, 34 semi-conductor producers and some 300 robotics competitors show how local rivals, each holding only a modest share of the home market, can prosper through rapid upgrading and global sales. The lesson to be learned from Japan is that competition works, not that we should limit it.[3]

The lesson from all this is that the best way to improve the performance of British industry is to expose it to as much competition as possible and to ensure that no local cartels can be created. The risk with government intervention is that it can create them. The evidence from our own economic performance in the 1980s shows what works. Industries facing increased competition from imports over the 1980s had a greater improvement in their own performance than those which did not. Free markets are indeed the route to prosperity.

CHAPTER X:

The Welfare State

Many people don't trust Conservatives with the welfare state. They believe Conservatives played no part in its creation. The popular assumption is that the welfare state was begun by the Liberals before World War One, despite opposition from the Conservative House of Lords who did not want to vote the taxes to pay for it. It was then expanded by the Labour government after World War Two, again despite opposition from groups then close to the Tory party such as the BMA. The conclusion they reach is that, really, the welfare state belongs to the Labour party or the Liberals; at best, Conservatives tolerate it and at worst they want to get rid of it.

The history of our welfare state is much more complicated and incremental than that. Conservatives have had their criticisms of the welfare state, and still do – as we shall see below. But equally, some of the leading Conservative politicians – including many on the right of the party – have contributed to its development. Joseph Chamberlain, the most dynamic if erratic Conservative politician of the last decade of the nineteenth century, was one of the first to advocate the old-age pension. His son, Neville Chamberlain, was the most effective ministerial expert on health and housing in the inter-war years. Enoch Powell, in the early 1960s, was probably our finest Minister of Health. Bevan had nationalized charitable and local government health services, but had no programme for investing in them – partly because of Beveridge's complacent assumption that as our health improved, spending on health care would fall. Powell was the first to see that the NHS could not just live on its pre-war inheritance but needed to expand and develop. Keith Joseph, as Secretary of State for Health and Social Services in the Heath government, presided over big reforms in health and social services, and raised the problem of the cycle of deprivation. The three great education reforms of this century – Balfour's Act of 1902 (extending public finance for Church schools), Butler's of 1944 (improving access to secondary education), and Baker's of 1988 (introducing the National Curriculum and giving schools the right to opt out of local authority control), are all Conservative. Indeed, historians will recognize 1988 as an *annus mirabilis* in the history of the welfare state, for that year also saw the review of the health service and the implementation of social security reforms.

Whatever the earlier history, it was believed that Thatcherites wanted to destroy the welfare state; the so-called 'savage cuts' of the 1980s were the means to this end. But the figures do not bear this out. Public expenditure on health, social services, education and social security stood at 20.4 per cent of the national income in 1979 and at 21.3 per cent of a much greater national income in 1990. There were, of course, intense political arguments about expenditure at the margin. Nevertheless the overall picture is clear: the 1980s saw big increases in spending – which more than kept up with the growth of the economy. Expenditure on the welfare state is, if anything, steadier under Conservative rather than Labour governments – under which it lurches from unsustainable spending sprees to financial crises and emergency cuts. (It is, for example, one of the iron laws of postwar government that spending on the National Health Service always rises as a percentage of national income under the Conservatives and falls under Labour.)

Although Conservatives have played such a leading rôle in the welfare state, and although expenditure carries on rising under Conservatives, many people believe the opposite. The explanation is very simple. Nobody is very clear *why* a Conservative should support a welfare state. It seems to fit in with the high-mindedness of the Liberals and the egalitarianism of the Labour party. But what is Conservative about it? If Conservatives do support it, is this mere political expediency? Maybe voters believe that when it comes to the welfare state, Conservatives are 'willing to wound, and yet afraid to strike'.

The Conservative approach often seems to boil down to two claims: only Conservatives know how to run the economy, and hence generate the wherewithal to finance the welfare state; and secondly, only Conservatives know how to manage it efficiently. Both claims are true but they lack any warmth or vision. They are the sort of things one says about something one does not really care for. Those boasts about extra expenditure can sound as if they are delivered through gritted teeth – like a husband telling his divorced wife how much alimony he is giving her.

We need to go back to first principles and face the fundamental question: why should Conservatives want a welfare state? Two general arguments are put forward first. Then opposing conservative and socialist views of the function of the welfare state in redistributing resources are contrasted. Finally we look at the conservative critique of the welfare state, yielding a distinctive view of how it should be formed.

Why Have a Welfare State: Efficiency and Community

There are two types of argument for a welfare state. Neither is exclusively conservative, but they both tie in closely with the two crucial elements of conservative philosophy – the belief in markets and the commitment to community.

The market argument for a welfare state is that it contributes to the successful working of a capitalist economy. The judicious provision of cash or services financed out of national insurance or general taxation can help the market to function. It is no accident that advanced Western economies are the ones which tend to have a welfare state. It is partly, of course, that only they are rich enough to afford one. But equally, the relationship goes the other way round – advanced Western economies need a welfare state in order to function. It is worth explaining why. Arnold Toynbee said: 'It is a great law of social development that the movement from slavery to freedom is also a movement from security to insecurity of maintenance.' The rural economies of primitive societies do not need a welfare state because, apart from natural disasters, they do not have the sudden losses of a cash income which create the need for one. Unemployment is a feature of economies with paid employment, economic cycles and continual change in patterns of production; indeed, the very term 'unemployment' first came into general political debate in the 1880s. Similarly, compulsory retirement at a fixed age is another concept which first emerged at the end of the nineteenth century.[1] The idea that there comes a specific age at which one can no longer carry out any economically useful work is a product of industrial capitalism. The development of unemployment benefit and retirement pensions contributes to economic efficiency by making it easier for firms to shed labour and to recruit new workers from a pool. Health care and education both raise the quality of a nation's 'human capital'. There are, of course, many other arguments for them too: saying they are useful is not to deny they have other virtues.

We may have explained the need for some of the fundamental services of the welfare state, but we still need to show why the state has such a big rôle in financing and organizing them. This is where the next stage of the efficiency argument comes in. If these are voluntary, private schemes they encounter the problem of adverse selection – the tendency to get the bad risks. As Winston Churchill explained: 'Voluntary schemes of unemployment insurance . . . have always failed because those men likely to be unemployed resorted to them, and, consequently, there was a preponderance of bad risks . . . which must be fatal to the success of the scheme.' At the same time, of course, the commercial insurers are trying to do the very opposite and only accept what they would regard as the good risks. The logic of this drives the government to intervene and require everyone to take out insurance at the same premium. At this point we are moving far away from normal commercial insurance and have, in effect, invented state-run national insurance.

The development of the welfare state can thus be seen, not as an interference with the free market but as helping to preserve it. A warning of what can happen if such developments are not permitted can be seen in the sad history of rent controls. In 1915 there was rioting in Glasgow in protest at rent rises. The government felt they had to do something for fear of social disturbance and disruption of the war effort. Had they been sensible, they would have invented housing benefit, helping poorer people meet the costs of commercial rents. Instead, they invented rent controls which avoided any welfare expenditure and simply regulated the rents charged by the landlord. Thus begins the sad history of interference in the free operation of the housing market. Instead of the generality of taxpayers explicitly bearing the cost of helping poor people with their rent, one specific group, landlords, had, in effect, some of their property expropriated. Public expenditure on expanding the welfare state through housing benefit would have been much more consistent with the free operation of the housing market.

These efficiency arguments are never convincing on their own, however. Housing benefit might be better than rent control, but what if we simply said we have no obligation to help people with their housing costs through either benefits or rent control? If they could extract enough pay from their employers to pay for their housing, all well and good; otherwise they could turn to relatives or to charities or be homeless. The efficiency argument could then be stated in an even more rarefied form: it is difficult for a homeless family to be fit, or for a homeless child to do well at school, and this, in the long run, is an economic cost – which makes it rational for us to step in.

Rather than develop ever more ingenious economic arguments for the welfare state, there comes a point when we really have to confront a simple moral obligation towards fellow members of our community. Regardless of whether people in need have been reckless and feckless or unlucky and unfortunate there comes a point when the exact explanation of how they became destitute ceases to matter. They have a claim on us simply by virtue of being compatriots. The welfare state is an expression of solidarity with our fellow citizens. As Enoch Powell argued in the 1950s, it expresses our sense of community. Moreover without these moral arguments it is difficult to see how the coercive taxation to finance welfare spending can be justified.

The market and the community arguments together explain the remarkable consensus in most advanced Western nations that some sort of welfare state is both necessary and desirable.

They explain why a Conservative can support the welfare state and also provide grounds for criticizing particular institutional arrangements if they are not living up to those principles. But because these two arguments are now such a fundamental part of the consensus of advanced Western countries, there is nothing distinctively conservative about them (though Conservatives may be more serious about applying these two criteria in practice than those on the left, who appear to back anything provided it is done in the name of the welfare state).

Mutual Insurance

It is when one turns to the rôle of the welfare state in redistributing resources that political differences emerge. For socialists the welfare state is perhaps the most powerful tool available to achieve their objective of equality. The welfare state is to be used to intervene in everyone's income and their access to health services and education so as to achieve 'social justice'. And because many people think this must be the rationale for the welfare state, they assume that anti-egalitarian conservatives must also be anti-welfare state.

There is a different view of the working of the welfare state. For the conservative it is an enormous mutual insurance scheme covering us all against ill-health, unemployment and loss of earning power in old age. At any one moment there is a redistribution from the contributors paying their national insurance and taxes, to the beneficiaries receiving their old-age pension or their free health care. Hence we think of the welfare state as redistributing resources to others. But if, instead, we think of our own relationship to the welfare state during our lives, it is clear that what it really does is to reallocate those resources through the different stages of the life cycle. In this way resources are taken from us when we are working, and we are given command over resources when we are being educated, or un-employed, or sick, or retired.

For the mutual insurance model to work successfully, two important conditions must be met. First, we must all feel our-selves likely to fall into some of the categories of need at some point. The welfare state is not a mechanism whereby *we* give to *them*, but a mechanism whereby *we all* get some protection in the face of life's costs and disasters. Winston Churchill put it very well when his wartime Coalition was planning the National Health Service, long before Aneurin Bevan got involved:

> The discoveries of healing science must be the inheritance of all. That is clear. Disease must be attacked, whether it occurs in the poorest or the richest man or woman simply on the ground that it is the enemy; and it must be attacked just in the same way as the fire brigade will give its full assistance to the humblest cottage as readily as to the most important mansion ... Our policy is to create a national health service in order to ensure that everybody in the country, irrespective of means, age, sex, or occupation, shall have equal opportunities to benefit from the best and most up-to-date medical and allied services available.[2]

A second requirement for this mutual insurance is that there should be little risk of moral hazard undermining the system. Moral hazard occurs when the very fact that an adversity is insured against makes us more irresponsible and thus more likely to get into adversity. Old age and the more acute manifestations of ill-health are not like this. Anxieties about the effects of the welfare state arise when these two conditions of mutuality and absence of moral hazard appear not to be met – as, for example, with some social security benefits.

Many countries have tried to capture this concept of mutual insurance in arrangements whereby people pay contributions earmarked for certain specific purposes. But there is no reason for it to take a specifically actuarial form with detailed calculations of contribution rates related to the likelihood of one's making any particular claim. Nor does the state need to set up some special accumulating fund. We can make our claims on future resources very effectively through the state's power to tax and raise insurance contributions. There is no point in setting up elaborate alternative mechanisms whereby a national insurance fund acquires shares (slowly nationalizing British industry) or government securities (which in turn pay interest financed out of taxes anyway). That is to pursue the analogy with commercial insurance to absurd extremes.

Perhaps now is the moment to give some space to the cynic jeering from the sidelines. He will say that he admires the modern conservative's ingenuity in thinking up arguments for the welfare state, but the fact is that radical Conservative thinkers and politicians of the postwar era have all been against it. Citing the likes of Neville Chamberlain and Winston Churchill will not do. What about the red-blooded Thatcherites?

That cynic might be referred to one of the New Right's key tracts – Hayek's *Constitution of Liberty*. He offers a clear rationale for the welfare state along the lines set out above:

> All modern governments have made provision for the indigent, unfortunate, and disabled and have concerned themselves with questions of health and the dissemination of knowledge. There is no reason why the volume of these pure service activities should not increase with the general growth of wealth. There are common needs that can be satisfied only by collective action and which can be thus provided for without restricting individual liberty. It can hardly be denied that, as we grow richer, that minimum of sustenance which the community has always provided for those not able to look after themselves, and which can be provided outside the market, will gradually rise, or that government may, usefully and without doing any harm, assist or even lead in such endeavours. There is little reason why the government should not also play some rôle, or even take the initiative, in such areas as social insurance and education, or temporarily subsidise certain experimental developments. Our problem here is not so much the aims as the methods of government action.[3]

Mrs Thatcher had a very similar view of the welfare state. After all, she began her ministerial career in 1961 as Joint Parliamentary Secretary to the Ministry of Pensions and National Insurance. The vision of the welfare state as mutual insurance was one which she herself shared. She did not see anything socialist in it – it was simply prudence.

There always has been a clear division between conservative and socialist on the question whether the welfare state should be seen as having a rôle in redistributing incomes in pursuit of equality in the guise of some idea of social justice. That was always the focus of criticisms of the welfare state from conservative thinkers such as Hayek and Enoch Powell. It is to that which we must turn.

The Welfare State as a Means of Achieving 'Social Justice'

Egalitarian socialists find the rôle of the welfare state as mutual insurance much too tame – they want to use it to achieve 'social justice' by redistributing resources to poorer people. The model is not the Pru, but charity (although compulsion means it lacks the same moral quality). Hayek again makes the point in his discussion of social security in *Constitution of Liberty*:

> Seen as an alternative to the now discredited method of directly steering production, the technique of the welfare state, which attempts to bring about a 'just distribution' by handing out income in such proportions and forms as it sees fit, is indeed merely a new method of pursuing the old aims of socialism. The reason why it has come to be so much more widely accepted than the older socialism is that it was at first regularly presented as though it were no more than an efficient method of providing for the specially needy. But the acceptance of this seemingly reasonable proposal for a welfare organisation was then interpreted as a commitment to something very different.[4]

This is the link between the egalitarianism at the heart of socialism discussed in Chapter VIII and the distrust of the Conservative record on the welfare state with which we began this chapter. The argument seems to go like this. People like the welfare state. They believe that its rationale is the pursuit of equality. Socialism is the party of equality. Therefore socialists must be the only people who can be trusted with the welfare state. A Conservative needs to challenge that chain of reasoning. Socialism is indeed largely about equality, but equality does not make much sense. Trying to rest the case for the welfare state on equality gives it distinctly shaky foundations. And what we like about the welfare state is not its supposed egalitarianism anyway, but its help to us through the life cycle and its commitment to helping other members of the community who are in dire need. Those are principles which any conservative can accept. Severed of its supposed connections with egalitarianism, the welfare state becomes a shared part of our national life and we can have political arguments about its scope and how best to reform it, without getting bogged down in arguments about first principles.

Some people, both on the left and the right, argue that the objective should be, wherever possible, to relate eligibility for the services of the welfare state to income. Why should the duchess collect child benefit, they ask. They might equally ask why the dowager duchess should get her old-age pension, and why the duke should be entitled to use the NHS. (That most people do not pose these further questions is evidence of their respect for the contributory principle.)

There are several conservative objections to this preoccupation with means testing. It cuts across the principles of efficiency and of community described above. It is economically inefficient to have a host of income-related tables and means tests which simply worsen the poverty trap. Imagine that if you got a job or started working overtime your family lost its entitlement to child benefit and health care, and your pension entitlement was reduced. It would be a terrible disincentive to personal advancement. Moreover, the communitarian picture of the welfare state reminds us that it is something we share – like the right to vote or the obligation to serve on a jury – and not something that divides 'us' from 'them'.

It was William Beveridge's insight that we can target welfare state spending by helping categories of people – such as the sick, the disabled or the very old – who are quite likely to be facing either lower incomes or higher living costs. Targeting does not require means testing. Those who put their faith in means testing are also ignoring the conservative insight that there is no fulcrum outside British society on which one can rest a lever for shifting it. The welfare state is not a mechanism for changing society, but a mirror reflecting it. If means tests are widespread, then prosperous, well-informed people start adjusting their financial affairs so they are still entitled to the means tested benefit – that has been the experience of Australia, which tried to means test the pension and found that within a decade many people had adjusted their affairs so as to gain entitlement to the new benefit. Nobody should be surprised that the welfare state takes on the character of the society within which it exists.

The Erosion of Institutions and Values

The conservative case for the welfare state outlined so far in this chapter does not mean that conservatives must just passively accept its expansion indefinitely. Conservatives have always had two crucial anxieties about the welfare state. First, that it could erode those independent 'mediating structures' which stand between the individual and the state – everything from the Victorian Friendly Societies through to, most importantly, the family. The second fear was that the welfare state erodes values of prudence, foresight and independence. These two arguments are, of course, closely related – after all, institutions embody our values and it is the values which sustain the institutions.

There is a progressive Whig history of the welfare state which begins with heroic individuals who identify a distinct social problem and try to address it by charitable work – from Octavia Hill and Josephine Butler in the nineteenth century through to Dame Cecily Saunders and Bob Geldof today. But this charitable work, like patriotism, is not enough. The critics say it is patchy and unplanned. So the planners come along and displace – indeed, even occasionally nationalize – these charities and instead we have a nationwide service provided by public-sector employees and financed out of taxation: they believe voluntary workers are like the pioneers on the American prairie – always followed by the railroad of the welfare state.

But a conservative wonders whether this always is progress. Is the meals-on-wheels service any better as the volunteers of the WRVS are replaced by the employees of local authority social services departments? Volunteers don't strike, but paid employees can. Would we expect the RNLI to be taken over by the coastguard?

There are perhaps two reasons why we attach such value to voluntary charitable activities. One is because they can meet needs which are beyond the welfare state and may often meet them better than a planned public-sector system can do. Their superiority partly lies in the greater variety and experiment enjoyed outside public-sector control. That is the way to make new discoveries about how best to provide welfare services.

There is another, deeper, reason for the value we attach to these non-state activities. They are reminders that we cannot simply discharge our duty to our fellow citizens by paying our taxes and letting government departments spend the money. Indeed, it is the paradox of the welfare state that whilst on the one hand it embodies our sense of solidarity with others, it can also alienate us from others. The person sitting in his cosy living room during a cold snap, wondering why the social services do not check on the old lady next door, epitomizes the price that we can pay for the welfare state.

All this ties in with the big issue in Chapter V – whether conservatives should put the emphasis on national community or on smaller communities. This may have appeared a highly theoretical question, but the debate about the rôle and limits of the welfare state shows its practical application. From the rôle of charitable endeavour, through to self-governing hospital trusts and the encouragement of private pensions in place of the State Earnings Related Pension Scheme (SERPS), the underlying question is the same. To what extent should our relations with our fellow citizens be directed by uniform, nationwide provision. The Conservative will always want to enhance the rôle of arrangements – voluntary, or private or simply local delivery of public programmes – which stand between the individual and the nation-state.

When it comes to education or health, two different functions are being carried out – financing the services and actually providing them. An arm's length relationship between purchaser and provider can ensure that these functions are much better carried out. The purchasing authority can decide what is in the interest of its customers without being preoccupied with the convenience of producers. It is the logic behind the internal market in the NHS, open enrolment in schools, competitive tendering for local authority services and John Major's Citizen's Charter. It shows that the conservative belief in competition and choice can be used to raise the quality of tax-financed public services.

It is not just a free-market argument; it relates to the conservative belief in particular communities and institutions. Schools and hospitals are precious institutions at the heart of a local community. They can and should command the loyalties both of the staff and of parents, pupils and patients. If they are free from elaborate bureaucratic control, they can develop their own distinctive characters; they belong to the neighbourhood, not to Whitehall. Fertile diversity displaces Fabian uniformity.

As the health and education reforms are implemented, they help to ensure that these institutions of the welfare state do indeed become Burkean little platoons. Instead of being subject to detailed centralized control, they become vehicles for local involvement. And that in turn helps to build up a much more intense feeling of engagement.

Of course the most important of all these mediating structures is the family. The job of the welfare state is to help the family but not to take over so many of its functions that we become, in effect, married to the state. At that point the erosion of the institution of marriage threatens some of our society's most crucial values. This is the argument that the welfare state erodes values.

It has been observed that 'in the past we used to suffer from social evils, now we suffer from our remedies for them'. Perhaps the most devastating critique of the welfare state – to be found, for example in Charles Murray's book *Losing Ground* – is that it undermines important social values. It wreaks this damage by giving short-term financial rewards to behaviour which is in the long term destructive both of the individuals involved and of the society at large.

This is really the moral hazard problem which was discussed earlier: measures you take to help people who have got into difficulties may make it more likely that more people will get into those difficulties in future. But this problem is not a conclusive case against welfare provision. Consider how we would drive if car insurance was not compulsory but prohibited. There would be fewer accidents but those which did occur would be financially catastrophic. We have decided that in this case, therefore, moral hazard is the lesser of two evils.

This dilemma reveals what one might call the paradox of integration at the heart of the debate about the effect of the welfare state on values. We provide money to people in need so they can afford to participate in the life of society. But if they become dependent on state finance and lose any sense of control over their own lives, they may not be really integrated into society after all. It was the great fear of the Victorians that the price of eliminating poverty was the spread of pauperism. This danger can never entirely disappear, but it is much reduced if we support a welfare state based on the principle of mutual insurance. Then it is clearly a device for helping us and our families through the life cycle.

CHAPTER XI:

Constitutional Change

Over the past few years the Great and the Good have showered down upon us a variety of proposals for changing our political and institutional arrangements: proportional representation, a Freedom of Information Act, a new written constitution, devolution, regional government, disestablishment of the Church of England, a new Bill of Rights, reform of the House of Lords, etc. Edmund Burke mocked the leading French purveyor of constitutions of his own time:

> Abbé Sieyès has whole nests of pigeon-holes full of constitutions ready made, ticketed, sorted, and numbered; suited to every season and every fancy; some with the top of the pattern at the bottom, and some with the bottom at the top; some plain, some flowered, some distinguished for their simplicity, others for their complexity; some with councils of elders, and councils of youngsters; some without any council at all. Some where the electors choose the representatives; others where the representatives choose the electors. Some in long coats, and some in short cloaks; some with pantaloons; some without breeches ... So that no constitution-fancier may go unsuited from his shop.[1]

But it will not do just to mock. It is worth investigating what is driving the current interest in constitutional reform. Four different considerations can be distinguished.

First, there is the simple opposition to Conservative policies. Some people so dislike Conservative governments, particularly ones which actually do things, that they can only conclude that it is some deep failing in the British constitution which has allowed Conservative governments successfully to pursue their policies. Some of the reformers do not like what a Conservative government does and want to make its life more difficult. Of course, some policies of Conservative governments have not

151

worked, notably the community charge. But that is no more evidence that the British constitution is in rags and tatters than was the ability of Labour governments to pursue nationalization through most of the postwar periods. All governments, even ones with impeccable democratic credentials, do silly things from time to time. That is not proof of some deep constitutional failure. And the community charge is going, without the constitution being transformed. Disagreeing with the substance of a government's policy is a very poor basis for planning constitutional reform.

The second factor behind the constitutional reform debate is the intellectual ascendancy of free-market economics. Those people who always want to have a project for intervening somewhere are no longer so confident of their ability to intervene in the economy. In the 1960s and 1970s they would have been writing national economic plans, preparing national investment strategies, and designing ever more sophisticated prices and incomes policies. But they know they have lost those arguments. They have retreated to the high ground of constitutionalism. The advantage for them of constitutional reform is that it does not interfere with the free operation of the economy and it does not appear to cost much. It does not show up on the economic balance sheet.

Thirdly, there are the modernizing practical men who argue that the constitution needs reforming so as to bring it up to the same standards as those of other advanced Western countries. This argument merits more serious attention than the previous two. We won our crucial freedoms earlier than other countries – looking back as far as the Glorious Revolution of 1688, if not to Magna Carta of 1215. But the reformers say we are now stuck at a particular stage of political development and have allowed other countries to overtake us. Just as some say that our economy is weak because we were the first to industrialize, so the argument is that our constitution is weak because we established political liberties whilst remaining a monarchy. As a result we are still subjects of a monarch, not citizens like the Americans or the Germans.

The Conservative reply to that is simply to ask: 'So what?' We have had a different history from the countries of the Continent and that does give our constitution a different shape from theirs. But that is not evidence that it is wrong. Different countries with their own traditions can quite reasonably have different constitutional arrangements. That the German constitution works well for them is no reason for us to have it here. They may be happy as citizens of a republic, but it is not for us. Why can we not happily accept the compromise on our passport in which one is described as a 'British subject: Citizen of the United Kingdom and Colonies'? The reformers have to show exactly what is wrong with our constitutional arrangements and that it can be set right without causing even worse problems.

The reformers have replied to this challenge with varying attempts at linking economic or political failure with what they regard as flaws in our constitutional arrangements. We were told during the 1970s that the so-called 'British disease' of low growth and high inflation went back to constitutional failings. We were supposed to suffer from 'ungovernability' as economic and industrial reform was essential but at the same time impossible. We were told that British governments lacked the confidence and credibility to push through the necessary reforms because they had not been elected by proportional representation. The corporatists said that our state was not properly developed and that vested interests such as the trade unions and the employers were not fully involved in the processes of government. All these grand constitutional arguments of the 1970s now seem as dated as bell-bottomed trousers and the kipper tie.

There was a very different analysis of the failings of our constitution during the 1980s. Then we were told that reform was necessary because government had become too strong. Governments were finding it too easy to push through too much of their programmes. There was a risk that government would abuse its power. Constitutional fashions which can change so quickly show how difficult it would be to design a new constitutional settlement that would last for decades, if not centuries. The practical men would be much better off addressing specific abuses rather than trying to implement over-arching schemes for reform.

There is a fourth reason for the heightened interest in the whole subject of constitutional reform which shows why, for some people, the piecemeal approach is just not good enough. These reformers would draw on the argument that markets erode communities (outlined at the beginning of Chapter VII) and apply it to our constitutional arrangements. If we are indeed more mobile and more rootless then, the critics say, we need to make explicit what was previously absorbed as part of our common culture. An unwritten constitution requires a network of shared understandings and attitudes to sustain it; maybe those no longer exist. The values embodied in the Established Church and the monarchy can no longer be simply assumed to be shared by all the Sovereign's subjects. New, more explicit constitutional arrangements are needed. Their ugly slogan could be 'Legislation replaces Socialization'.

If this all sounds too abstract, consider an example from the 1980s. The City used to be largely self-regulating with shared conventions about how one should behave maintained by the long traditions of leading City families and firms. This came under increasing pressure during the 1980s because of the number of new players who arrived from outside the old City Establishment. It was a Conservative government which argued that we needed a new statutory framework for financial services – hence the elaborate Financial Services Act of 1986 and the long rulebooks prepared by the new self-regulatory organizations. The constitutional reformers would say that the arguments which applied to the City in the 1980s apply more generally to the country as a whole. If our economy and society are 'Americanized', then, as for the Americans, everything has to be written down and open to legal dispute.

A conservative has three responses to this line of argument. Firstly, our shared culture, and the institutions which embody it, may be more robust than the critics imagine. The hold on the popular imagination of the monarchy, the sovereignty of Parliament, even, at times of national crisis or rejoicing, the Church of England, is greater than the reformers recognize. The most serious domestic threats to our great national institutions are the corrosive effects of economic failure (particularly inflation) and the devaluation of authority caused by excessive government intervention. Provided we avoid those perils, our political culture, and the institutions which sustain it, can survive.

Secondly, those institutions work more subtly than the reformers recognize. They have seen us through an extraordinary variety of economic and political crises and they have always held. This flexible strength derives from the nature of our constitution. It is not, despite the cliché, an unwritten constitution. It is a dispersed constitution, written down in hundreds of places. It can be found in parliamentary legislation governing the workings of the legislature, executive and judiciary. It can be found in the rules of parliamentary procedure and, of course, in our courts' interpretation of the common law, handed down in a continuous series of written judgements. It is like a coral reef, living and changing. That makes it much more sophisticated than any one fixed constitutional document could ever be.

Thirdly, there is a contradiction in the reformers' argument. On the one hand they say that our existing constitutional arrangements cannot be sustained because we are now a pluralist, multicultural society. Yet they also maintain that if only some miscellaneous group of retired politicians, political scientists and eminent lawyers got together they could write a constitution which would command widespread assent. Why should those experts command greater authority than our long-established and loved institutions?

Of course we can admire countries which have written out a new constitution and then made it work. The two most heroic examples are undoubtedly the American Constitution of 1787 and the German Basic Law of 1949. Those are two great success stories. One pre-condition for their success was the total destruction of a previous constitutional arrangement, making the explicit re-creation of political order a sad necessity. But to assume that we could somehow replace our constitutional traditions with a new set of arrangements in peacetime without any crisis flies in the face of all historical evidence.

The closest that we came to such a radical constitutional transformation was the Glorious Revolution of 1688. It was that which finally established what is our central constitutional principle – the sovereignty of the Monarch in Parliament. We can divide constitutional reformers into the fundamentalists and the realists, depending on whether they reject or accept that principle.

The fundamentalists wish to step outside our entire political tradition and establish, through a written constitution or perhaps a special Bill of Rights, mechanisms which limit what future parliaments can do. Whilst the traditional constitutional convention is that Parliament cannot bind its successors, what these fundamentalists are saying is that we now are to bind our successors somehow. They are arrogantly assuming that the present must be better than both the past and the future. It is exactly the opposite of a conservative view which would both respect the constitutional traditions which have brought us thus far, and would also recognize that they may change further in the future in ways in which we cannot now guess. It is difficult to conceive, indeed, how – short of enormous historical rupture – we could reach the circumstances in which the sovereignty of Parliament was constrained in this way. (The argument that Europe is already doing so is considered in Chapter XII.)

The realists, by contrast, understand that the British constitution is perpetually being modified as we change the laws regarding the working of the executive, the legislature and the judiciary. Some of these rules may become obsolescent and new rules may be needed – as Bagehot observed at the end of *The English Constitution*:

Our law very often reminds one of those outskirts of cities where you cannot for a long time tell how the streets come to wind about in so capricious and serpent-like a manner. At last it strikes you that they grew up, house by house, on the devious tracks of the old green lanes; and if you follow on to the existing fields, you may often find the change half complete. Just so the lines of our Constitution were framed in old eras of sparse population, few wants, and simple habits; and we adhere in seeming to their shape, though civilisation has come with its dangers, complications, and enjoyments. These anomalies, in a hundred instances, mark the old boundaries of a constitutional struggle. The casual line was traced according to the strength of deceased combatants; succeeding generations fought elsewhere; and the hesitating line of a half-drawn battle was left to stand for a perpetual limit.[2]

Only the most absurd reactionary could possibly maintain that all these rules must now remain fixed for ever more. The question is whether, pursuing Bagehot's image, we approach them with the impatience of some postwar town planner and tear down the fabric we have inherited, or whether we instead settle for a judicious programme of improvements. Conservatives must always be willing to contemplate practical improvements.

The two proposals for ambitious constitutional reform which have greatest popular currency at the moment are a new Bill of Rights and electoral reform. These are considered in turn.

A New Bill of Rights?

We do already, of course, enjoy one Bill of Rights – the one which was passed into law in December 1689 after the Glorious Revolution. It emerged from a supreme moment of constitutional crisis, after the Commons had declared the throne vacant with the flight of James II. But even then our predecessors managed to transform our political arrangements within the framework of the sovereignty of the Monarch in Parliament. The Bill of Rights is, legally speaking, simply another Act of Parliament which could be repealed by Parliament if it wished. Yet it has helped preserve our freedoms for over three hundred years. It refutes the argument that our freedoms can only be properly protected if somehow the principle of parliamentary sovereignty is constrained.

The Bill of Rights is not a grand declaration of constitutional principles but a set of limited measures declaring certain specific abuses to be illegal and enumerating certain 'freedoms'. The abuses which are listed include suspending Parliament, levying money, and the raising of a standing army in time of peace if any of these are done without consent of Parliament. Among the freedoms set out are (in the words of one historian):

That elections of members of parliament should be free; that freedom of speech and proceedings in parliament should not be impeached or questioned out of parliament; that excessive bail should not be demanded; that jurors in trials for high treason should be freeholders; that it is the right of the subject to petition and, lastly, that for the redress of grievances, parliament should be summoned frequently.[3]

Such specific measures are, to quote Dicey: 'worth 100 constitutional articles guaranteeing individual liberty'.

The British Bill of Rights reflects the conservative insight that it is very difficult to make sense of the idea of the *rights of man* as some abstract concept removed from a nation's historical experience or its political practices. But we can make sense of the *rights of British men and women*. It may be difficult to make sense of the abstract idea of *freedom*, but we can understand the *freedoms* which we enjoy in our historic national community and which are embodied in our constitutional practices. We often assume that specific provisions must rapidly become out of date but general statements last for ever. Our Bill of Rights shows the opposite to be true. If it had set out what a typical MP of 1689 thought were the rights of the British people, it would now be an interesting period piece. Its detail has guaranteed its longevity.

But we now must turn from the peaks of British constitutional achievement to contemporary arguments about the constitution. Advocates of a new Bill of Rights must obviously maintain that somehow our freedoms are under threat. Organizations with names such as Charter 88 implied, with their reference to the Czechoslovak Charter 77 Movement, that somehow we were edging towards East European oppression. Actually, of course, the opposite was happening. The East Europeans were looking to us as an example of how to enjoy freedom. However offensive the comparison with the old Eastern bloc, apparently well-intentioned people seem to have believed that the British people during the 1980s were suffering under some sort of dictatorship. We need, therefore, to look at the record of that decade and compare it with the 1970s.

We were prepared during the 1970s to tolerate quite remarkably intrusive government intervention in our economic affairs. These were not just economic nonsenses, they were serious constraints on personal freedom. For example, exchange controls were so tight that you used to have to take your passport to the bank to collect your allocation of £50 worth of foreign currency before travelling abroad. That is the sort of measure which dictators use in order to stop people fleeing abroad.

Another example was the attempt by the Callaghan government to run a prices and incomes policy without any parliamentary backing for it. Attempts were made to enforce it by the notorious operation in 1978 of sanctions against firms which gave pay settlements higher than the government thought right. The government operated a 'black list' with no legal basis whatsoever. Firms would be denied access to export credits. Industrial grants would be withheld. Contracts for public-sector work would be lost. It was an outrageous example of executive discretion in pursuit of a policy which had no legislative backing at all.

If we look at the record of the 1980s, by comparison, it is clear that the British approach of achieving constitutional reform by specific legislative improvement was followed with energy and success. The list of constitutional reforms is quite considerable. The Data Protection Act of 1984 allows everyone access to information held about them on computer records, except for those concerning crime, tax and national security. There is a right for an individual to see his file and insist on changes if the material is incorrect. The Police and Criminal Evidence Act of 1984 gives judicial protection to journalists' notebooks. The Criminal Justice Act of 1988 sets out new, more rigorous rules on treatment of suspects, as well as allowing the press to challenge specific orders restricting their reporting. The Security Service Act of 1989 at last put the security service on a statutory footing and in the words of the then Home Secretary 'for the first time, provides a mean of redress for a citizen who thinks that he has a cause for grievance against the service.'[4] The Official Secrets Act, also of 1989, strips 'away the criminal law from the great bulk of official information so that budget secrets, draft White

Papers on health, correspondence dealing with pension decisions will no longer be subject to an Official Secrets Act'.[5]

All this adds up to an authentically Conservative programme of constitutional reform entrenching people's rights through specific legislative measures. It is the way in which policy must develop further in the 1990s. John Major's Citizen's Charter, for example, promises new rights of access to information about the performance of the public sector and these may well require statutory backing. That is the right way forward.

There is one seductively simple way of implementing a new Bill of Rights which has many eloquent advocates – the incorporation of the European Convention on Human Rights into British law. The British government signed the original European Convention on Human Rights in 1951. Since 1966 individuals have had the right to petition the European Court of Human Rights (which is quite distinct from the European Court of the European Community). The government is committed to implementing the court's judgements. But British judges cannot take account of the European Convention on Human Rights when reaching their decisions. That is why some eminent lawyers, such as Lord Scarman, have long argued that we should actually incorporate the Convention into British law so that the principles of the European Convention could be interpreted by our own judges. They argue that this would also reduce the number of occasions when we were hauled before the European Court of Human Rights for breaches of the Convention.

This is an attractive argument, but it has some difficulties. First of all, the European Convention on Human Rights is, necessarily, drawn in very broad terms. John Patten, the Minister at the Home Office who has written and spoken with great authority on the whole subject of constitutional reform,[6] has compared the specific rights of someone accused of an offence in a British court with Article 6 of the European Convention on the rights of a person charged with an offence. That has no reference to the time limits before they come to justice, no rules on cautions, nothing specific on court and police procedures. Any British citizen accused of an offence would be much better off looking to specific British legislation than to the vague terminology of that Convention. This is the familiar argument in favour of specific statutory protections rather than grandiose statements of principle.

It leads on to a further tricky issue. If we incorporated the European Convention into our own legislation, our judges would have responsibility for interpreting these broad principles in specific circumstances. That would be a big change for the British judiciary. There is a risk that judicial appointments would become highly political, as everyone would wish to know how different judges were likely to interpret the European Convention. It is fallacious to take judges as they currently behave and ask that they carry on enjoying their current obscurity, their relatively high degree of confidence, their political independence – and yet at the same time to give them very different powers. If their powers change then other features of the post will also change. The current arrangements might give us the best of both worlds. Individuals can appeal to the European Court of Justice, so there is a body of judges interpreting rather general principles and acting as a long-stop. But because the Convention is not directly incorporated into our law, there is a *cordon sanitaire* around it so that our own judges do not become embroiled in such interpretation.

Proportional Representation

The argument about electoral reform is a good example of the observation at the beginning of this chapter that constitutional arguments can be driven by straightforward political considerations of self-interest. By and large, parties which are in office do not see any good arguments for changing the electoral system which got them there. And after a chastening period in opposition, parties often become convinced that it is only the unfair electoral system which is keeping them out of office. As it is the Liberal Democrats who now advocate proportional representation (PR), it is ironic that when we got quite close to it – in 1918 – it was opposed by the majority of Liberals, including Lloyd George who described it as a 'device for defeating democracy, the principle of which was that the majority should rule, and for bringing faddists of all kinds into Parliament, and establishing groups and disintegrating parties'.[7]

There are two different kinds of argument for PR which need to be distinguished. One argument is that it is fair; the other argument is that it yields more effective government.

It is tempting to dismiss the fairness argument simply and robustly. Britain is an advanced Western country in which it is obvious to any outside observer that we enjoy representative democratic government as one would expect in such a country. Modern democracies have a variety of electoral arrangements with party lists, first ballots and second ballots, electoral colleges, multi-member constituencies, as well as first past the post. The British electoral system is a perfectly respectable member of this family of electoral systems. Any political party could if it wished identify specific features of our system which do not treat it 'fairly'. For a Conservative it is, for example, the over-representation of socialist-voting Scotland in Parliament (it has seventy-two MPs, as against fifty-eight if its constituencies were as populous as in the rest of the UK). The shrinking inner-city areas of England which return Labour MPs also get more weight than the increasingly populous Tory shires and suburbs. Thus the Conservative party won more votes than Labour in the general election of February 1974 yet Labour had more MPs and there was a (minority) Labour government. But any set of rules must inevitably yield some hard cases. The important point is that, over all, they should be coherent and legitimate.

The advocates of proportional representation point out that most European countries do have an element of PR in their electoral systems – though not America or Japan. They claim that this shows we are falling short of an ideal to be found on the Continent. But a comparison of the different electoral systems on the Continent shows that there is no single, agreed type of proportional representation. Indeed, the advocates of different forms of PR all tend to denounce other versions as vehemently as they do the first past the post system. Undoubtedly the purest, and in a sense fairest, form of PR would be a straightforward party list with the number of seats allocated exactly in accordance with the percentage of national vote won by each party.

The trouble with this system is that it gives great power to the party machine and severs any connection between elected politicians and particular constituencies. In practice, therefore, continental electoral systems tend to be mixed – partly list, partly first past the post and constituency-based.

British advocates of proportional representation tend to favour the single transferable vote (STV) in which each elector has one vote which can be reallocated to second or third preference candidates if the elector's first choice is already home and dry. It was invented by Thomas Hare in the middle of the nineteenth century and was dubbed the 'Hare-brained Scheme'.[8] Winston Churchill dismissed it because it would mean that MPs were elected 'by the most worthless vote given to the most worthless candidate'.[9] It is a much more unusual system than the one we have at the moment. No major country uses it. It does keep a constituency-based electoral system, though the constituencies are much larger than we are used to and have several MPs. The only reason it features so prominently in British debate is the Liberal Democrats' fear that any other form of PR would mean their becoming a 'list party' with many of their MPs lacking links to a constituency.

All the arguments about fairness would resurface in a battle about the exact make-up of seats. Smaller constituencies would favour the existing party over the one which currently comes a close second. Larger, multi-member constituencies would yield a much greater variety of political representation. So the argument about fairness would then become an intricate one about the right size for a multi-member constituency.

If the pursuit of fairness is so inconclusive, what about the other argument – that government will be more legitimate and hence more effective if we have PR? One very important consequence of PR is that no one political party of itself would be likely to have enough MPs to form a government on its own. In changing our electoral system we would have changed fundamentally our style of government. Thereafter we would probably have coalition government, which could be along German lines, with two large parties of the left and right, and a smaller centre party holding the balance of power. Thus government is determined by the centre party's decision on which of the larger parties to support. It is not obviously superior or more democratic or more effective than the British system of changing governments. An alternative is that one, or both, of the large parties could collapse into smaller factions. This is what has happened to the right in France and to the left in Italy. This in turn can lead to periods of electoral domination by one large party (possibly in alliance with some of the tiddlers). But that is precisely one of the complaints which the advocates of PR make about the current British system.

Some of the advocates of proportional representation maintain that it will improve our whole pattern of government. But our electoral system may just reflect back at us deeper features of our society. If a country is very cohesive already, then it can probably make any reasonable electoral system work. If it is already very fissile, then no amount of ingenious electoral reform is likely to give its politics greater coherence.

It is not obvious, therefore, that proportional representation is either going to end up with a more fair way of choosing governments than what we have at the moment, nor that those governments will be any more effective. In those circumstances, perhaps it is best to stick to the current arrangements. It was the Marquess of Salisbury who used a good Conservative argument to dismiss PR because he felt that 'it was not of our atmosphere – it was not in accordance with our habits; it did not belong to us . . . it belonged to the class of impracticable things'.[10]

The Abuse of Human Rights in the United Kingdom

This chapter has largely been concerned with traditional conservative defences of our current constitutional arrangements against some schemes for reform. But that is not to imply that we have no constitutional problems to address. Everything is not for the best in the best of all possible worlds. It is just that the advocates of reform, with their grandiose schemes, are in danger of ignoring particular abuses of the rights of people living in the UK. A conservative analysis of the failings of our constitution would draw lessons from the two most conspicuous and outrageous causes during the 1980s. That is where practical reform is needed.

The first specific problem is obviously the series of cases in which people were wrongly convicted of terrorist offences or murder and our system of judicial appeal failed to correct the injustice. Lord Runciman's Royal Commission is currently studying these miscarriages of justice. It should lead to suggestions for the improvement of the operation of the appeal system to try to reduce the risks of such failures in the future.

But perhaps the most shocking misuse of the rights of our fellow citizens in Britain in the 1980s was the notorious child abuse scares, notably in Cleveland and the Orkneys, in which children were removed from their families. Throughout the UK during the 1980s, innocent parents suffered the sudden knock on the door at dawn with their children taken away, and only recovered them after months of legal wrangling. Legal safeguards were not met and procedures intended to protect families were ignored. The lesson to be drawn from such cases was that there was a culture in the social services, and amongst some doctors, which was quick to assume abuse and not interested in the legal safeguards of the rights of families.

This shows the connection between these two injustices of the 1980s. One reason why the innocent Irishmen and the innocent families suffered so much was that the police and social workers were so confident that they were right, that the normal rules of procedure seemed like a tiresome impediment to 'true' justice. The police thought that they knew that those men were guilty, and extracting the confessions from them, and tampering with the evidence, was simply to ensure that the court reached the 'right' judgement. Social workers thought they knew that the children were being abused, and the finer points of legal procedure were simply standing in the way of their addressing a monstrous evil. Any society needs to erect barriers in the way of such impetuousness and the most effective ones are so robust, ancient and ivy-clad that they are part of the way we think. It is indeed our culture which sustains our liberties.

That leads us on to what is perhaps the most important point about the protection of our rights and our liberties. No amount of ingenious legislation, no constitution however well designed, is of any use unless we enjoy what Michael Oakeshott called 'the political economy of freedom'. It is the rich and varied life of a civil society which best protects us:

> Liberties, it is true, may be distinguished, and some may be more general or more settled and mature than others, but the freedom which the English libertarian knows and values lies in a coherence of mutually supporting liberties, each of which amplifies the whole and none of which stands alone. It springs neither from the separation of church and state, nor from the rule of law, nor from private property, nor from parliamentary government, nor from the writ of *habeas corpus*, nor from the independence of the judiciary, nor from any one of the thousand other devices and arrangements characteristic of our society, but from what each signifies and represents, namely, the absence from our society of overwhelming concentration of power. This is the most general condition of our freedom, so general that all other conditions may be seen to be comprised within it . . .[11]

That is why political refugees have fled to our country over the centuries, coming often from places with the most elaborate constitutional provisions on human rights, to one with no such written constitution. They knew where their freedoms were more secure.

CHAPTER XII:

Europe

Conservatives are uneasy about the development of Europe. We might like to join in the rhetoric about boldly creating an exciting new federal Europe. But the reality is that any conservative is afraid that things which he most values – ties of national identity and affinity – are threatened by the consolidation of the European Community (the EC). Continental political parties – of the left and right – seem much easier with this prospect and the rhetoric which goes with it; that in itself shows the significant difference between our political culture and those of the Continent.

The Germans only emerged as a unified state under Bismarck and had a terrible history in the first half of this century. They know that their neighbours are very wary of a powerful German state at the centre of Europe. For that reason they offer to tie themselves down in a wider European identity. In Foreign Minister Genscher's words, Germany must 'embed our national interest in the European interest'. When Germans talk of federalism they are not, therefore, intending it as a threat to the nationhood of others, but as a gesture of friendship – saying that Germany is prepared to lose itself in a greater whole.

The particular institutions of the French state tend not to survive for very long. France gets through republics the way that Hollywood stars get through marriages. The intense national pride felt by a Frenchman has very little to do with the institutions of the Fifth Republic or any respect for the French political process: it is more to do with culture and cuisine, than with the vagaries of political institutions. More recently, the French socialists have had to fill the vacuum caused by the abandonment of their domestic socialist agenda within two years of their taking office in 1981. The project of building Europe was an exciting substitute for a defunct domestic political agenda.

The European Community began as an instrument of Franco–German reconciliation; that it is now the pre-eminent European political institution is a genuine and legitimate source of pride to both countries.[1] By contrast, the institutions on which we have pinned our hopes during the postwar period, from EFTA (the European Free Trade Area) to the Commonwealth, have proved embarrassingly weak. NATO (the North Atlantic Treaty Organization) is our only conspicuous success, and perhaps for that reason we hear few complaints about loss of independence because of those Treaty obligations.

Anyone wishing to see how a country manages without any serious government at all, should study Italy. The results can be delightful. But for the Italian governing élite it is rather unfortunate that they have virtually no authority. In particular it is awkward that they do not have a tax system which enables them to raise anything like enough funds to finance their public expenditure. For the Italians, therefore, Brussels offers the prospect of some viable government as a substitute for domestic ungovernability.

The British case is different. We have a much longer history of stable political culture and established institutions than any of the continental countries. The British economy may have performed poorly since World War Two, and some reformers may find our constitutional arrangements unsatisfactory and out of date. Nevertheless our institutions fit us like a comfortable old suit which has been with us through many an occasion.

Not only does the British nation-state have a longer history than many on the Continent, but that history is much more closely tied up with a specific set of political institutions. In particular, the sovereignty of the Monarch in Parliament is a fundamental part of the British historical tradition. The Palace of Westminster is a much more vivid symbol of British nationhood than the German or French assemblies. The currency in which we are to pay for so-called 'European Political Union' is much more precious for us than for some other EC states. Continental countries may be used to written constitutions which constrain what their representative assemblies do; we are not. Political sovereignty matters more to us than to many continental countries; it is more closely linked to our sense of nationhood. But the two concepts are different; they need to be distinguished. And our own history makes it more difficult for us to do this than some other EC countries.

Has our membership of the EC led to a fundamental loss of sovereignty? Parliament has certainly ceded powers in a way that has never been done before. If UK domestic legislation clashes with EC legislation then the courts now treat EC legislation as paramount – because the European Communities Act, passed when we joined the Community in 1972, requires this of them. Sir Geoffrey Howe cites a case which makes this clear: in 1989, the government passed an Order in Council reversing the previous year's legislation on fisheries policy which conflicted with EC law.[2]

But Parliament still cannot bind its successors. Any future Parliament could vote to withdraw from the EC, and it seems extremely unlikely that the other members of the EC would force us to stay. There is no reference to secession in the Treaty of Rome but the EC is a long way from having its President Lincoln. Anyway, the EC does not have any military power or even any criminal law, as against civil sanctions. Thus, on the crucial test of reversibility, there has been no fundamental loss of sovereignty – it may have been put into a blind trust, but it can always be reclaimed.

What matters more than arguments about sovereignty is our sense of nationhood. The real conservative fear must be that our sense of Britishness, even, dare one say it, our Englishness, is eroded by the EC. Nationhood is a cultural and historical concept. Vita Sackville-West captured it when she wondered what might have been in the heads of the assembled peers waiting in Westminster Abbey for the coronation of George V in 1910:

It is to be doubted whether one person in that whole assembly had a clear thought in his head. Rather, words and their associations marched in a grand chain, giving hand to hand: England, Shakespeare, Elizabeth, London; Westminster, the docks, India, the Cutty Sark, England; England, Gloucestershire, John of Gaunt; Magna Carta, Cromwell, England.[3]

Those associations remain intense and real even though they have slowly changed: the docks have been transmuted into Docklands; India has gone.

Powerful forces are at work gradually changing our sense of nationhood. The EC is but a small part of this process. We are becoming more cosmopolitan. Five times as many UK residents travelled abroad in 1988 as in 1968, and came back with a taste for different food or some appreciation that there were other ways of doing things, which changed our tastes. One of our greatest cultural achievements, our language, has been, paradoxically, too successful. It is now so universal that it is beyond our own control. If you speak French you are probably French; if you speak German you are probably German. There is only a remote chance that you are British if you are speaking English. A vigorous English literary tradition would now carry on even if all the inhabitants of the British Isles were wiped out. The Church of England has played a crucial historic rôle in our identity as a Protestant island off a largely Catholic Continent. Now, on a typical Sunday, more Roman Catholics go to church in the UK than do Anglicans. That suggests that our history since the Reformation is anyway taking a turn back towards the Continent.

The Conservative must certainly recognize that British nationhood does not now mean what it meant a century ago. The question is how these changes affect the nation-state. Does it remain, in either sense of the word, vital? The answer is that it does, but not necessarily carrying out the same range of functions as twenty or fifty or a hundred years ago.

The Nation-State and the Internal Market

Europe presents the dilemma of markets and communities, the theme of this work, in its most vivid contemporary form. It is tempting for any Conservative to pretend it is all very straightforward. Modern Conservatives support what used to be called the Common Market – the free movement of goods and people – and oppose Brussels-based corporatism. Similarly, Conservatives will support European co-operation but oppose the absorption of Great Britain into a 'United States of Europe'. These two approaches were neatly combined by Mrs Thatcher when she said: 'We have not successfully rolled back the frontiers of the State in Britain, only to see them reimposed at a European level with a European super-state exercising a new dominance from Brussels.' What more needs to be said?

A lot more. Conservative opposition to a corporatist Europe is obvious. It requires fighting many difficult battles in Brussels, but the objective is clear. What is interesting and important is a conservative view of a free-market Europe, the sort of Europe envisaged in the 1992 programme. That forces the Conservative to face the question of whether the nation-state itself is the ultimate supply-side constraint (a phrase I owe to Anthony Teasdale), to be swept away by the tide of free trade.

The classic nation-state, as developed during the nineteenth century, both constitutes a well-defined free-trade area and ties the participants in that market together in a shared, historic community. It works because it combines economic mobility within its borders with, at the same time, a strong sense of cultural rootedness. It reconciles markets and communities.

Each nation-state might pursue a policy of free trade with other nation-states but this was always a matter of policy, not an inescapable constitutional constraint. A genuine European Community internal market, with free movement of goods, services, people and capital, offers a deeper conception of free trade, enforced by a supra-national judge.[4]

In a traditional free-trade area, anything which satisfies the regulatory requirements of the British government can be sold in Great Britain, even if it is made in, say, Germany. Similarly, anything can be sold in Germany which meets German regulatory requirements, even if it is made in Britain. All through the 1960s and 1970s the European Commission worked within this framework. The only way forward seemed to be to harmonize German and UK domestic regulations on an agreed EC standard. This approach to harmonization made the European Commission a laughing stock. But it was actually an attempt to acknowledge the rights of nation-states, who were being asked in effect to formulate a new national rule which would also apply in all other EC states.

The internal market programme following from the Single European Act of 1986 moves on from classic free trade to what might be called 'deep' free trade. Lord Cockfield's bold launch of the internal market programme in 1985 rested on the much more ambitious view that if a product or service meets the requirements of any member state of the EC, then it can be sold in any other member state of the EC. This approach cuts the Gordian knot of elaborate harmonization negotiations by settling for mutual recognition instead. If cassis de Dijon is good enough for the French to drink, then it is good enough for Germans as well (the original *cause célèbre* on which this policy of mutual recognition rests). This 'deep' free trade is closer to the clause of the American Constitution which says that there shall not be any interference with inter-state commerce. Unlike classic free trade, this approach requires mutual trust in each other's regulatory standards – if a bank is acceptable to the Greek authorities, then it can set up in London as well. It also gives us a much greater and legitimate interest in the policies of other countries. It is a massive erosion of the traditional prerogatives of the nation-state.

There is a second crucial difference between old-style free trade and the EC internal market – the European Commission and the Court of Justice act as prosecutor and judge to enforce open markets. There is no such supra-national authority behind GATT (the General Agreement on Tariffs and Trade of 1947). If the French government tries to stop a British firm from exporting to France, then that firm can apply to the European Commission for fair treatment from the French. One of the most dramatic examples of this policy is in government aid to industry. No individual national government is going to police its own aid; instead, they can police each other within the EC by mutual jealousy – a much more effective discipline. The Commission then requires individual nation-states to recover subsidies which it considers to be a distortion of the market.

Some argue that it is possible to have a free-market Europe, modelled on EFTA (European Free Trade Association, 1960) or the recent US/Canada Trade Agreement, which are supposed to bring all the advantages of open markets without the constraints on national governments imposed by the Single European Act. That is too good to be true. There is no ingenious structure which avoids the twin issues of mutual recognition and supranational enforcement described above. The current EFTA countries have been trying for years to develop some external association with the EC which escaped the problem of loss of national control, but it cannot be done. EFTA countries have been offered open access to the EC without becoming full members provided they accept EC standards for everything from financial institutions to professional qualifications. In that case, they would be conceding a considerable loss of national control without any corresponding rôle in the decision-taking of the EC. They have now realized how unpalatable that option is and therefore several EFTA countries have applied to join the EC.

Whatever its imperfections in practice, it is clear that the internal market is a genuine extension of the free market for goods and services, people and capital; and it is also a substantial constraint on the powers of individual nation-states. Setting aside all the arguments about corporatism, and fears about future European developments, the internal market programme itself is a real constraint on the British government and Parliament; it reflects a big change in the powers and responsibilities of nation-states. It is surprising that Conservative anxieties about the development of a 'United States of Europe' have been prompted by the risk of a single currency, and not by the Single European Act which was signed in 1986 with so little criticism from within the Conservative party.

Monetarism and Patriotism: EMS and EMU

In 1971 the Bretton Woods system, which had linked the world's currencies to the dollar, and the dollar to gold, since World War Two, collapsed. From 1971 to 1976 British economic management was conducted without any financial framework, either international or domestic, for maintaining the soundness of the currency. At the IMF's insistence, in 1976 we introduced our own domestic monetary rule, restricting the rate of growth of the money supply and thus protecting the value of the currency. The decision to join the Exchange Rate Mechanism (ERM) of the European Monetary System (EMS) in October 1990 took us back to a pre-1971-type system of fixed exchange rates (as discussed in Chapter IX).

But exchange rates in turn need some anchor, otherwise all the countries linked in the exchange rate system can simply suffer high inflation together. Under the Bretton Woods system that anchor was the link between the dollar and gold. Now it is Germany's domestic monetary rules which provide that essential discipline. Britain has not abandoned monetary targeting so much as contracted it out to the Germans. Instead of running our own domestic monetary rules, which we have found difficult to do successfully, we have tied ourselves to the Germans' monetary rules – because they have a much better record in conducting monetary policy.

Some critics see this on its own as a regrettable loss of monetary independence – indeed, of monetary sovereignty. But for any anti-inflation strategy to be credible, the government has to forswear, publicly and convincingly, the right to depreciate its own currency. Only then do all the different economic agents adjust their behaviour to fit in with the rules. To this extent any serious monetary policy involves the government in relinquishing its sovereign power to debase its own currency. But equally, any rule – be it domestic or external – is voluntarily chosen by the government and could in principle be abandoned however unpalatable that might be. In this respect the ERM is just like the old Bretton Woods system.

There are good Tory arguments why it might be better to have an external exchange rate rule than domestic monetary targets. Exchange rates are more comprehensible and command the attention of the layman in a way that esoteric rules for domestic monetary growth cannot. Even Mrs Thatcher, who was sceptical about the ERM, was inclined to demand action from the Treasury if the newspaper headlines were screaming that the pound was plummeting against the dollar or the Deutschmark. Despite the fact that many of the advocates of our membership of the ERM have dizzy hopes of creating a closer European Community, in practice the ERM works because of its appeal to nationalist instincts. Exchange rate rules harness patriotism in support of monetarism.

The real anxiety is whether the ERM is but a step towards European Monetary Union. The Americans never saw the Bretton Woods system as a step towards one world currency but Jacques Delors does argue that the ERM is but the first stage towards a single European currency. His arguments are essentially political. One of the fundamental attractions of the ERM – linking other European currencies to the robustly anti-inflationary Deutschmark – is seen by the sensitive souls of the European Commission and the French government as somehow deeply embarrassing. Rather than accepting that this is a sensible, comprehensible and robust framework for their financial policy, they instead want to dilute the German dominance by giving the job to a new, Europe-wide monetary institution.

There are obvious practical objections to the Delors approach. It is a dangerous gamble because, in effect, we abandon fixed, Europe-wide exchange rates in favour of one Europe-wide domestic monetary target. Instead of the Germans running a monetary policy and the rest of us linking ourselves to them – a very sensible form of specialization of effort in financial policy – we would have a single European currency with Europe-wide targets for the growth of the ecu. That is technically a much more difficult task than the Germans running their own monetary policy over a much smaller and more cohesive economy and the rest tying ourselves to that. It also loses the clarity and emotional force of exchange rate rules. Interest rates would be determined on a Europe-wide basis by the need to keep the growth of the ecu within its target range. But should we have a narrow definition of the ecu – maybe simply 'currency in circulation' – or have a broader definition, which would include bank deposits in all EC countries? We would in effect be returning to all the esoteric arguments which dogged British monetarism during the 1980s, but on a Europe-wide level. And it does not tie in neatly with our political culture; suffering high interest rates in defence of a target for growth of the ecu would not be something that any politician would wish to try to explain to the electorate.

Given the crucial importance of credibility, predictability and authority in the conduct of monetary policy, dramatic institutional change is particularly risky in this area. But that is precisely what the advocates of a single European currency want. They do not want Europe's anti-inflation policy to rest any longer on the Bundesbank with its long and successful history of holding inflation down and its unrivalled international respect. Instead there is to be a new body, a European central bank, probably composed of the leaders of the individual national central banks. This new body will not be able to operate as successfully as the Bundesbank has done. For the Germans to imagine that this problem can be solved by simply putting upon the new bank a legal obligation to maintain the value of the ecu is unusually naïve. The new bank will not have the habits of thought, the balance of political power, the track record necessary for it to have credibility. That credibility will have to be earned in a long and painful process – as we in Britain have seen from our attempts to regain it in the 1980s, having thrown it away in the 1960s and 1970s. Any new institution will look more like the Bundesbank, the more it is restricted to an élite of low-inflation members. In that case, the French will have failed in their objective of diluting the Deutschmark zone.

The neat reply to these doubts is to say that Europe can only move to a single currency after its economies have converged so closely that the final step is virtually trivial. But it all depends on what convergence means. Just as any ambitious shifts of political decisions to Brussels require first the spread of a deep Europe-wide political culture, so economic convergence would also have to rest on a deep, shared, economic culture. The alignment of inflation rates and the disappearance of exchange rate adjustments are not enough. The crucial question is how flexibly real resources can be moved around the EC. What happens if the oil price falls and oil companies pull out of Aberdeen? Do the people of Aberdeen pile their possessions into their station-wagons and drive to Dusseldorf to find work? That is the basis of the economic convergence enjoyed in the USA – it is sustained by significant rates of internal migration. Rates of internal migration within the EC are still much too low to permit such economic convergence. A crucial step to achieve it would be to harmonize on one language – English being the obvious candidate. But for some reason this is one element of European harmonization not proposed by the Commission.

Even if all the economic issues set out above could be resolved, there still remains the fear that a single European currency means loss of sovereignty. But the crucial test of sovereignty is reversibility. Although there would be considerable technical difficulties, it would still be possible for the United Kingdom's Parliament to resolve that it wished to take back the management of its own currency into its own hands and to re-create the pound sterling as a distinct currency separate from the rest of the EC.[5] We would retain the right of monetary secession just as we would retain the right to political secession. Sovereignty which has been voluntarily renounced and can be regained has never been truly lost.

The real question is what happens to our nationhood in these circumstances. If we share one currency with the people of Frankfurt and Lyons and Milan, are we also sharing citizenship with them? Certainly, moves towards one currency such as, for example, Germany's economic and monetary union in 1990 and the old Anglo–Scottish monetary union, are closely associated with political union as well and there would be powerful pressures for further integration of other policies – fiscal policy, for example, and regional policy – which would be a significant further erosion of independent nationhood. Indeed, some rules on fiscal policy are essential for a single currency to work. Usually the fiscal power is aligned with monetary power – the individual states of America spend less than the federal government and local authorities in Britain spend less than central government. A system where the monetary authority lay with the new European bank, but most of the public expenditure and tax decisions were with the nation-states, would be unstable. There would be an obvious temptation for individual nation-states to run large budget deficits, confident that stability of their international currency would protect them from the inflationary consequences. The consequences of individual national fiscal laxity would thus be dissipated across Europe. The European bank would have to hold interest rates at a higher level than would otherwise be necessary and we would suffer lower rates of growth throughout the EC. Fiscal policy rules would therefore follow quite closely along with monetary policy rules. We would have moved a long way to establishing one Europe-wide economic policy.

The Future of the European Community

British diplomacy has oscillated between splendid isolation from the affairs of the Continent and passionate, constructive engagement. A hundred years ago, when Britain was at the height of its powers relative to the rest of the world, we had no continental commitments or alliances. Just over fifty years ago, during World War Two, Churchill was willing to offer complete union between France and Britain in a desperate attempt to hold the line against Germany. Later on he talked about a 'United States of Europe'. Some Conservatives conclude that the Paris–Bonn axis running the EC is so strong and exclusive that we should either opt out entirely or become what might be described as 'semi-detached' members of the Community. But the real challenge, which is surely in the tradition of British diplomacy for most of our history, is to participate effectively in European negotiations so that it becomes unthinkable that the EC should embark upon a major policy initiative with which we are in fundamental disagreement – the privileged position now enjoyed by Germany and France. As John Major has said, we must be 'at the heart of Europe'.

There are three elements to a Conservative agenda for Europe. Each of them stands as a contrast to the nightmare of a Europe aiming at socialist corporatism and sliding into division and national conflict.

First, there is the objective of creating a genuine internal market in which people, capital, goods and services can move freely around the Community. That is not going to be in place on 31 December 1992. It will absorb the political energies of the leading European States for the rest of this century. And this agenda of 'deep' free trade must inevitably involve some constraints on national governments, as shown above.

Moreover, it will drive social and cultural integration. One of the main themes of this book has been that markets bring people together. They help create and sustain communities. The internal market will help bring the European Community together. If people within the EC work wherever they like, if qualifications earned as a dentist in Liverpool enable one to practise in Marseilles, and if we experience the same volume of internal migration as in America, then further development in Europe's political and economic arrangements may become possible in the future.

It would, however, be a terrible mistake for the European Community to embark upon grandiose schemes of political, economic or monetary integration without the underlying political culture or economic convergence necessary to sustain them. That would mean that Europe risked setting up fragile institutions which could not bear the pressure placed on them from national political and economic interests. The debate in Brussels would not be between left and right but between different countries fighting for their own clearly perceived national self-interest.

The second element to the Conservative vision of Europe has to be limited government. Socialists believe that the internal market is not a good thing in itself but a pill which has to be sugared by ambitious new programmes of regional subsidies and social aid. But such an approach would again threaten to blow Europe apart. It would set Europe on a downward spiral in which the central authority could offer such tempting prospects of regulatory favouritism, or public expenditure, that the different component nations would engage in a vicious battle fought at the federal level. Instead of the mutually beneficial and integrative experience of the market, there would be the corrosive and destructive zero-sum game of big government. A corporatist Europe with national political cultures would destroy itself.

There is nothing wrong with national diversity and, indeed, national competition. That is what has given Europe its vigour over the centuries. It is only if these rivalries are fought out in an over-regulated economy that they become destructive. Europe needs a variety of social and economic arrangements. We have now learned from the environmentalists that the world needs its rich and varied genetic bank in order to survive. We need to sustain different breeds of plants and animals so that even if one falls prey to a new virus, or a change in tastes, others can come in to fill the gap. But just as we need bio-diversity, so we also need national diversity.

The pursuit of uniformity is supposed to ensure a 'level playing field' as if we are creating a Europe of which the most fastidious groundsman could be proud. But competition does not require that the teams be identical – they can be coached differently and play differently. Europe's historic strength is that it is a continuous experiment in which different social and economic arrangements can be compared.

Finally, the European Community must move from being the pre-eminent political institution of Western Europe to being the pre-eminent institution covering all of Europe. That means being open to enlargement from the prosperous countries of Scandinavia, together with Switzerland and Austria. It also means being open to the new democracies emerging from the old Soviet Empire – particularly Hungary, Czechoslovakia and Poland. Europe should not become so preoccupied with intensifying its own federalist arrangements as to make the entrance of these other countries more difficult. This is not to say that enlargement should be used simply as a device to stop federalism; enlargement is a good thing in its own right. Enlargement will bring new federalist pressures of its own – more majority voting, for example. But it is clear that ambitious regional policy or social policy commitments stand in the way of the opening up of the European Community. That would be a tragedy. What it might mean instead is a multi-speed Europe, or a variable geometry Europe in which different member-states participate in different sets of policies, chosen from an à la carte menu.

It is this Conservative vision of Europe which is both achievable and more attractive than visions from the wilder shores of federalism.

CONCLUSION

Conservatives appear to speak in two different languages. On the one hand they appeal to the individual, to initiative, enterprise and freedom. On the other hand there is the trust in community, deference, convention, authority. Many believe that these represent two fundamentally incompatible views of the world and that a set of free-market arrivistes have taken over the party of deference and authority.

Chapters I to IV showed that both approaches can be traced right back to the origins of conservatism. Edmund Burke, eloquent in his defence of tradition, was also the free-market follower of Adam Smith. Disraeli, who invented the idea of Empire, never allowed it to interfere with the principles of free trade. The One Nation Group of the postwar period not only accepted the principles of the welfare state, they also argued against government intervention in the economy. Mrs Thatcher never accepted the crude simplicities of *laissez faire* – she understood we had moral obligations to others.

Chapters V to VII attempted a philosophical rather than an historical approach to the reconciliation of markets and communities. Those libertarians who just believe in a world of free markets have no real account of the sources of our personal identity. That means they cannot properly explain integrity – what it means to be true to oneself and one's conscience. For them, we only accept the rules of the marketplace because of the external constraint of authority – there is no inner voice. It is why highly individualistic societies can end up with a high burden of regulation and intrusive government.

On the other hand, if we just appeal to the values of community, we find ourselves exposed to a different set of problems. Conservatism can descend into nostalgia. It becomes the political branch of society for the preservation of ancient monuments. It has no account of why tradition should be respected nor how we distinguish between the good and bad in our society.

Conservative thought at its best conveys the mutual dependence between the community and the free market. Each is enriched by the other. It is the point at which modern conservatism comes close to the most sophisticated liberalism. Hayek is a good example. Although he famously denied that he was a Conservative, his essay 'Individualism: True and False' shows such an awareness of the weakness of most progressive liberal ideas of the individual that it must be regarded as a classic Conservative text.

This preoccupation with linking communities and markets is part of a continuing Conservative concern with national integration. Disraeli's two nations, Salisbury's fears of national disintegration, the One Nation Group, John Major's opportunity society – all address the question of how to ensure that all British citizens feel that they participate in national life.

It is a fine point of political judgement, indeed of political principle, how much to expect us to share with our fellow citizens. Socialists are too ambitious: their egalitarianism was shown in Chapter VIII to be wrong in principle as well as destructive in practice. Nor can one expect any longer, if one ever could, uniformity of belief to weld us into one moral community – the nation as a monastic order writ large. Those extreme communitarians, like socialists, demand too much. We have to rub along together on these islands and that requires tolerance of diversity.

It is also wrong to demand too little – the libertarian error. Without shared loyalties to institutions we lose any basis of legitimacy for the state. Our shared historic culture is the most powerful force for national integration. Education can give everyone and anyone access to our literary and historical tradition. It is a sad irony that those progressive thinkers so keen to criticize Thatcherite individualism and the privatization of industry – where it makes obvious sense – have themselves encouraged the privatization of our culture. Look at the changes in a typical school curriculum over the past thirty years and one can see the fracturing of our literary tradition as the trivial and the meretricious jostle alongside the great. Similarly, a sense of the shape of our history has been lost, to be replaced by a miscellany of themes and special subjects. No longer can we be confident that someone emerging from our schools will have come across the novels of Charles Dickens or know who Winston Churchill was. As Prince Charles rightly observed, that is indeed cultural disinheritance. It is real deprivation. The battle for educational standards is perhaps the most important single battle for a Conservative to fight.

Chapters IX to XII looked at some current topics of political debate against the backgound of this concern with national integration. A market economy with low inflation, a welfare state in which we all share, and prudent constitutional reform are all part of the successful working of a modern free society. Any sensible Conservative attends to such arrangements. The threat to our precious national life comes from those on the left who try to do too much – giving government a rôle in detailed management of the economy, using the welfare state as an instrument of egalitarianism, or transforming our constitution. More recently we have seen a new threat from those who want to create a federal Europe, developing EC institutions beyond the underlying economic and cultural integration necessary to sustain them.

Limiting the power of government is essential in holding us together as a nation. We need to be permanently on our guard against the temptation of arguing that if something is bad, it should be illegal; and if something is good, it should be subsidized. We do not want to live in a country in which everything which is not forbidden is compulsory. If we all are perpetually fighting to take resources from others, or to coerce others, using the state as our weapon, then we will indeed experience national disintegration. Edmund Burke set out the argument as well as anyone:

> It is one of the finest problems in legislation, and what has often engaged my thoughts whilst I followed that profession, 'What the state ought to take upon itself to direct by the public wisdom, and what it ought to leave, with as little interference as possible, to individual discretion'. Nothing, certainly, can be laid down on the subject that will not admit of exceptions, many permanent,

some occasional. But the clearest line of distinction, which I could draw, whilst I had my chalk to draw any line, was this; that the state ought to confine itself to what regards the state, or the creatures of the state, namely, the exterior establishment of its religion; its magistracy; its revenue; its military force by sea and land; the corporations that owe their existence to its fiat; in a word, to everything that is *truly and properly* public, to the public peace, to the public safety, to the public order, to the public prosperity. In its preventive police it ought to be sparing of its efforts, and to employ means, rather few, unfrequent, and strong, than many, and frequent, and, of course, as they multiply their puny politic race, and dwindle, small and feeble . . . as [statesmen] descend from the state to a province, from a province to a parish, and from a parish to a private house, they go on accelerated in their fall. They *cannot* do the lower duty; and, in proportion as they try it, they will certainly fail in the higher. They ought to know the different departments of things; what belongs to laws, and what manners alone can regulate. To these, great politicians may give a leaning, but they cannot give a law.

. . . the leading vice of the French monarchy . . . was . . . a restless desire of governing too much. The hand of authority was seen in everything, and in every place. All, therefore, that happened amiss in the course even of domestic affairs, was attributed to the government; and as it always happens in this kind of officious universal interference, what began in odious power, ended always, I may say without an exception, in contemptible imbecility.[1]

This judicious and limited government is crucial in holding us together as a nation. It creates space for the free market to operate. As we saw in Chapter VI, the market works precisely because we are different – we have different skills and different tastes. It successfully integrates people with different plans and skills in such a way that we all help to serve each other's purposes. It is the most powerful device for human co-operation that one can envisage. A shared cultural tradition, limited government, the free market, the welfare state and loyalty to the central institutions of the nation-state, are the integrating forces in which a conservative trusts.

It is self-indulgent of us to imagine that these big issues in political thought have somehow risen for the first time in the twentieth century. The reconciliation of rational calculating economic man with co-operative social man was at the heart of eighteenth-century thought. The argument about national integration was a live one throughout the nineteenth century which had to face such issues as Catholic emancipation and the problems of an urban underclass. Indeed, the rapidly industrializing Britain of the nineteenth century faced these problems in a more acute form than we do now. That was when the population flocked from the countryside to the town. And then there was not the stabilizing influence of a large number of elderly people – Victorian England was a much more rootless and youthful culture than our own.

In a sense, then, the Conservative party has always been modernizing, it has always been addressing political questions arising as a result of political and economic change. It has never been simply the nostalgia party. But in that case what is special about the modern conservatism of the postwar period? It was only then that conservatism properly came to terms with the economic and social changes of the twentieth century. The inter-war drift of the party was towards economic intervention and corporatism. It was a world in which it was thought planners could control the economy like technicians sitting in front of an array of dials at a power station. The postwar Conservative party saw that there was a rôle for the public sector in the welfare state, but not in detailed micro-economic intervention.

At a more abstract level, the party responded to the advance of socialism by becoming the party of freedom. And this was not just a principled defence of British freedoms and the rights of property. It also appealed to a mass electorate because freedom worked. It was a means to enjoy greater economic prosperity. As Burke said:

I shall always, however, consider that liberty as very equivocal in her appearance, which has not wisdom and justice for her companions; and does not lead prosperity and plenty in her train.[2]

The Conservative party's achievement is to show how apparently contrasting political principles can in practice be reconciled. Individualism and tradition can be reconciled because we have a tradition of individualism. Standing by traditional Conservative principles is reconciled with the need to offer the prospect of prosperity to a modern democratic electorate because freedom is the way to prosperity. The tension between market and communities is resolved because they help to sustain each other. In addressing these issues Conservatives place themselves at the heart of the British political tradition.

BIBLIOGRAPHIC NOTE

The best introduction to conservatism is through the classic texts such as: Edmund Burke, *Reflections on the Revolution in France* (ed. Conor Cruise O'Brien), Penguin, 1986; David Hume, *A Treatise of Human Nature* (especially Book III) (ed. Selby-Bigge and Nidditch), OUP, 1978; David Hume's *Essays, Moral and Political*, OUP, 1963; Adam Smith, *The Wealth of Nations*, Books I–III, Penguin, 1986; Viscount Hailsham, *The Conservative Case*, Penguin, 1959; Friedrich Hayek, *The Constitution of Liberty*, Routledge, 1960; Michael Oakeshott, *Rationalism in Politics and other Essays*, Methuen, 1962; Michael Oakeshott, *On Human Conduct*, OUP, 1975.

The rest of this note follows the chapter headings of the book, recommending reading of particular interest. In order to keep the list to manageable proportions, there are no biographies.

CHAPTER I

Sydney Checkland, *British Public Policy, 1776–1939*, CUP, 1983 and Gertrude Himmelfarb, *The Idea of Poverty: England in the Early Industrial Age*, Vintage Books, 1985 are good accounts of changes in thinking about the rôle of the state after Adam Smith. M. Pinto-Duschinsky, *The Political Thought of Lord Salisbury, 1854–1868*, Constable, 1967 and Herbert Spencer, *The Man versus the State*, Liberty Classics, 1981 are useful introductions to two interesting late-nineteenth-century thinkers.

CHAPTER II

A mammoth guide to British political thought and culture over the past 150 years is W. H. Greenleaf's *The British Political Tradition*. Volume II, *The Ideological Inheritance*, Methuen, 1983, covers conservative and socialist political thought in the twentieth century. Matthew Fforde, *Conservatism and*

Collectivism, 1886–1914, Edinburgh University Press, 1990 is a revisionist account of conservatism at the turn of the century, emphasizing its principled objection to the growth of the state. Robert Colls and Phillip Dodd (eds), *Englishness: Politics and Culture, 1880–1920*, Croom Helm, 1986, dissects ideas of national identity and its relationship to the political debate of the time. Gertrude Himmelfarb, *Marriage and Morals among the Victorians and other Essays*, Tauris, 1989, includes illuminating essays on Bloomsbury and the thought of Michael Oakeshott.

CHAPTER III

The best two historical accounts of conservatism after World War Two are Nigel Harris, *Competition and the Corporate Society: British Conservatives, the State and Industry, 1945–1964*, Methuen, 1972 and Andrew Gamble, *The Conservative Nation*, Routledge & Kegan Paul, 1974. Samuel Brittan, *Steering the Economy: The Role of the Treasury*, Penguin 1971, is the authoritative account of economic policy in the first part of the postwar period. The Heath government must now be due for serious historical appraisal: a good short history is Dennis Kavanagh's essay on Edward Heath in Hennessy and Seldon (eds), *Ruling Performance: British Governments from Attlee to Thatcher*, Blackwell, 1987. Harris and Sewell, *British Economic Policy, 1970–74: Two Views*, Institute of Economic Affairs, 1975, contains a powerful attack on the Heath government's economic record and the most sophisticated defence of it.

CHAPTER IV

Peter Jenkins, *Mrs Thatcher's Revolution*, Cape, 1987, is the best book on the politics of the late 1970s and early 1980s – although he has more of a feel for the Labour party and the Alliance than for Conservatives. Dennis Kavanagh and Anthony Seldon (eds), *The Thatcher Effect*, OUP, 1989 is one of the best books on the Thatcher government's policies. Two attempts to analyse Thatcherism by writers associated with *Marxism Today* are thought-provoking: Andrew Gamble, *The Free Economy and the*

Strong State, Macmillan, 1988, and Hall and Jacques (eds), *New Times: The Changing Face of Politics in the 1990s*, Lawrence & Wishart, 1989.

CHAPTER V

The communitarian critique of liberalism is most accessible in Michael Sandel (ed.), *Liberalism and its Critics*, Blackwell, 1984. See also Alasdair Macintyre, *After Virtue: A Study in Moral Theory*, Duckworth, 1985. Hegel's *Philosophy of Right* (translated with notes by T. M. Knox, OUP, 1967) is the most ambitious attempt to set the conservative belief in a civil society richly endowed with mediating institutions into a rigorous philosophical framework. A good and accessible account of his thought is Charles Taylor, *Hegel and Modern Society*, CUP, 1979. Karl Mannheim's long essay on 'Conservative Thought' in *Essays on Sociology and Social Psychology*, 1953, is one of the best twentieth-century accounts of how Conservatives think. Roger Scruton, *The Meaning of Conservatism*, Macmillan, 1984, emphasizes a conservative commitment to the national community.

CHAPTER VI

A stimulating short essay on Adam Smith's thought is Donald Winch, *Adam Smith's Politics*, CUP, 1978. Samuel Brittan, *A Restatement of Economic Liberalism*, Macmillan, 1988, is a marvellous account of the subject. Arthur Seldon's *Capitalism*, Blackwell, 1990, is a wide-ranging if shallow review of free-market thinking; unlike Brittan, he lacks any interest in the philosophical questions posed by economic liberalism.

CHAPTER VII

David Miller's *Philosophy and Ideology in Hume's Political Thought*, OUP, 1981 is a clear introduction to Hume, probably the greatest conservative thinker of them all. Donald W. Livingston, *Hume's Philosophy of Common Life,* University of

Chicago, 1984, is more thought-provoking; it is the best attempt at a coherent conservative interpretation of Hume's history and his philosophy. John Gray, *Hayek on Liberty*, Blackwell, 1984, is probably the best account of Hayek's thought. J. A. Schumpeter, *Capitalism, Socialism and Democracy*, Unwin, 1943, is the most distinguished version of the argument that capitalism will fail because it succeeds. Albert O. Hirschman, *Exit, Voice, and Loyalty*, Harvard University Press, 1970, links economics and political science to give a very interesting account of different types of participation and market power.

CHAPTER VIII

One of the few conservative books attacking the idea of equality head on is Keith Joseph and Jonathan Sumption, *Equality*, Murray, 1979. J. R. Lucas has published two rigorous articles on the subject, 'Against Equality', *Philosophy* (XL), 1965, and 'Against Equality Again', *Philosophy*, 52, 1977. Isaiah Berlin has written a classic paper, 'Equality', *Proceedings of the Aristotelian Society 1955–56*, pp. 301–26.

CHAPTER IX

Christopher Johnson, *The Economy under Mrs Thatcher, 1979–1990*, Penguin, 1991, is a good recent account of economic policy in the 1980s.

CHAPTER X

The clearest account of the economic efficiency arguments for the welfare state is to be found in Nicholas Barr, *The Economics of the Welfare State*, Weidenfeld & Nicolson, 1987. John Hills (ed.), *The State of Welfare: The Welfare State in Britain since 1974*, OUP, 1990, looks at how the welfare state fared under the Thatcher government. The most thought-provoking conservative critique of at least part of the welfare state is Charles Murray, *Losing Ground: American Social Policy 1950–80*, Basic Books, 1984.

CHAPTER XI

The obvious starting point for any consideration of constitutional questions is still Walter Bagehot, *The English Constitution*, Fontana, 1963. The arguments for constitutional change are put powerfully by Vernon Bogdanor, *The People and the Party System*, CUP, 1981, and Nevil Johnson, *In Search of the Constitution*, Pergamon, 1977. A recent defence of a much more cautious approach to constitutional change is John Patten, *Political Culture, Conservatism, and Rolling Constitutional Change*, Conservative Political Centre, 1991.

CHAPTER XII

The best account of the significance of the internal market is Nicholas Colchester and David Buchan, *Europe Relaunched: Truth and Illusions on the Way to 1992*, Economist Books, 1990. A good short introduction to the development of the EC is William Wallace, *The Transformation of Western Europe*, Royal Institute of International Affairs, 1990. Ernest Gellner, *Nations and Nationalism*, Blackwell, 1983, is a lively series of essays on the whole question of nationalism.

CHAPTER 1

1. J. B. Bloch, *...was...volt di Superstition Political Centre*, 1956, pp. ... in Sui Price Shan, ...

2. See Robert Blake, *The Conservative Party from Peel to Thatcher*, Fontana, 1985, and the study by Sean Green, *The Tory Party 1880 to 1912*, OUP, 1995, emphasizes the strength of Toryism through to the middle of the twentieth century, at least.

3. The expansion here is round back to ...

4. Edmund Burke, *Reflections on the Revolution in France*, Penguin, 1968, p. 183.

5. Quoting Gertrude Himmelfarb, ... in *The Early Industrial Age*, Faber, 1985, p. 6].

6. Norman Gash, *Aristocracy and People: Britain 1815–1865*, Edward Arnold, 1979, p. 106.

7. Benjamin Disraeli, *Sybil*, Penguin, 1980, p. ...

8. The best book about this aspect of Disraeli is M. Pinto-Duschinsky, *The Political Thought of Lord Salisbury 1854–1868*, Constable, 1967.

9. Charles Dickens, *Hard Times*, Penguin, 1969, p. 145.

10. Herbert Spencer, "The Coming Slavery," in *The Man versus the State*, Liberty Classics, 1982, p. ...

11. Herbert Spencer, Postscript to the New Toryism, ibid., p. 30.

12. Quoted in Robert Taylor, *Lord Salisbury*, Allen Lane, 1975, p. 80.

13. Ibid., p. 73.

NOTES

CHAPTER I

1. T. S. Eliot, *The Literature of Politics*, Conservative Political Centre, 1955, pp. 13–14.
2. See Robert Blake, *The Conservative Party from Peel to Thatcher*, Fontana, 1985, pp. 1–9. Jonathan Clarke's *English Society 1688 to 1832*, CUP, 1985, emphasizes the strength of Toryism through to the middle of the eighteenth century, at least.
3. The expression can be traced back to a footnote to Chapter VII of John Stuart Mill's *Considerations on Representative Government* which refers to 'Conservatives . . . being by the law of their existence the stupidest party', Everyman, p. 261.
4. Edmund Burke, *Reflections on the Revolution in France*, Penguin, 1986, p. 181.
5. Quoted in Gertrude Himmelfarb, *The Idea of Poverty: England in the Early Industrial Age*, Vintage Books, 1985, p. 43.
6. Norman Gash, *Aristocracy and People: Britain 1815–1865*, Edward Arnold, 1979, p. 106.
7. Benjamin Disraeli, *Sybil*, Penguin, 1985, p. 96.
8. The best book about this aspect of Salisbury is M. Pinto-Duschinksky, *The Political Thought of Lord Salisbury, 1854–1868*, Constable, 1967.
9. Charles Dickens, *Hard Times*, Penguin, 1969, p. 145.
10. Herbert Spencer, 'The Coming Slavery' in *The Man versus the State*, Liberty Classics, 1981, p. 43.
11. Herbert Spencer, 'Postscript to the New Toryism' in ibid., p. 30.
12. Quoted in Robert Taylor, *Lord Salisbury*, Allen Lane, 1975, p. 80.
13. Ibid., p. 73.

14. Ibid., p. 82.
15. Michael Oakeshott, 'On Being Conservative' in *Rationalism in Politics and other Essays*, Methuen, 1962, p. 170.

CHAPTER II

1. Sydney Checkland, *British Public Policy, 1776–1939*, CUP, 1983, p. 180.
2. Robert Skidelsky, the leading historian of the period, attributes the remark to Tom Johnson, a rather more obscure member of the MacDonald government.
3. J. M. Keynes, *Memoirs*, pp. 97–8, quoted in Gertrude Himmelfarb, 'A Genealogy of Morals' in *Marriage and Morals among the Victorians and other Essays*, Tauris, 1989, pp. 34–5.
4. Irving Kristol, 'The Adversary Culture of Intellectuals' in *Reflections of a Neo-Conservative*, Basic Books, 1983, p. 27.
5. The source of the figure for the voting behaviour of unemployed people is the Harris/ITN exit poll. The source for voting intentions of teachers in higher education is a survey by MORI in *The Times Higher Education Supplement*, 5 June 1987.
6. Shirley Letwin, *The Pursuit of Certainty*, CUP, 1965.
7. Ibid., p. 350.
8. M. A. Hamilton, *Remembering my Good Friends*, p. 260, quoted in W. H. Greenleaf, *The British Political Tradition*, Vol. II: *The Ideological Inheritance*, Methuen, 1983, p. 382.
9. Quoted in Norman and Jeanne Mackenzie, *The First Fabians*, Weidenfeld & Nicolson, 1977, p. 406.
10. Malcolm Muggeridge, *Chronicles of Wasted Time*, Vol. I, p. 151, quoted in W. H. Greenleaf, op. cit., p. 407.
11. William Hazlitt, 'On Prejudice' in *Selections from the Writings of William Hazlitt*, ed. Alexander Ireland, Chandos, 1889, p. 348.
12. Stanley Baldwin, *On England*, quoted in Frank O'Gorman, *British Conservatism*, Longman, 1986, p. 181.
13. Quoted by Alan Beattie, *Political Quarterly*, 1973, p. 279.
14. L. D. Gammans, *Facing the Facts*, quoted in W. H. Green-

leaf, op. cit., p. 257.

15. *The Economist*, 2 April 1938, quoted by Nigel Harris, *Competition and the Corporate Society: British Conservatives, the State and Industry, 1945–64*, Methuen, 1972, p. 54.

16. Harold Macmillan, *The Middle Way*, Macmillan, 1966 edn, p. 11.

CHAPTER III

1. F. A. Hayek, *The Road to Serfdom*, Routledge & Kegan Paul, 1944, p. 159.

2. W. H. Greenleaf, *The British Political Tradition*, Vol. II: *The Ideological Inheritance*, Methuen, 1983, p. 310.

3. Quoted in Samuel Brittan, *Steering the Economy*, Penguin, 1971, p. 197.

4. Harold Macmillan, 'Twenty Years After' in *The Middle Way*, Macmillan, 1966 edn, p. xxii.

5. Viscount Hailsham, *The Conservative Case*, Penguin, 1959, p. 59.

6. One Nation Group, *Change is our Ally*, Conservative Political Centre, 1954, pp. 96–8.

7. *One Nation: A Tory Approach to Social Problems*, Conservative Political Centre, 1950, p. 18.

8. One Nation Group, op. cit., p. 7.

9. Nigel Harris, *Competition and the Corporate Society: British Conservatives, the State and Industry, 1945–64*, Methuen, 1972.

10. S. E. Finer, *Anonymous Empire: A Study of the Lobby in Great Britain*, 1958, quoted in Harris, op. cit., p. 73.

11. Hennessy and Seldon (eds), *Ruling Performance*, Blackwell, 1987, pp. 233–4.

12. Ibid., p. 227.

CHAPTER IV

1. Interview, *Woman's Own*, 31 October 1987.

2. The full figures for voters aged 18 to 29 are: 1983: Conservative 39 per cent; Labour 32 per cent; Alliance 25 per

cent. 1987: Conservative 36 per cent; Labour 35 per cent;
Alliance 26 per cent. Source: Harris/ITN exit polls.
3. Edmund Burke, *Reflections on the Revolution in France*, Penguin, 1986, p. 90.

CHAPTER V

1. T. S. Eliot, 'Notes towards the Definition of Culture' in *Selected Prose*, Faber, 1975, p. 298.
2. Ibid., 'Tradition and the Individual Talent', p. 38.
3. Blackpool Conference speech, 11 October 1991.
4. Edmund Burke, *Reflections on the Revolution in France*, Penguin, 1986, p. 135.
5. Quoted in Karl Mannheim, 'Conservative Thought' in *Essays on Sociology and Social Psychology*, ed. Paul Kecskemeti, Routledge & Kegan Paul, 1953, p. 140.
6. Letter to the Galatians, 3:28.
7. F. W. Nietzsche, *Twilight of the Gods*, quoted in Gertrude Himmelfarb, *Marriage and Morals among the Victorians and other Essays*, Tauris, 1989, p. 23.
8. Michael Oakeshott, *On Human Conduct*, OUP, 1975, p. 188.
9. Ibid., p. 321.
10. *The Times*, 21 January 1991.
11. Nigel Andrews, *Financial Times*, 20 December 1990.
12. Gertrude Himmelfarb, op. cit., p. 228.
13. See Peter Berger, 'On the Obsolescence of the Concept of Honour' in Michael Sandel (ed), *Liberalism and its Critics*, Blackwell, 1984.
14. Thomas Carlyle, 'Gospel of Mammonism' in *Selected Writings*, Penguin, 1986, pp. 277–8.

CHAPTER VI

1. Adam Smith, *Wealth of Nations*, Penguin, 1986, Book II, Ch. 3, pp. 441, 443.
2. Ibid., Ch. 5, p. 461.
3. Joseph Schumpeter, *Capitalism, Socialism and Democracy*, Unwin, 1943, p. 67.

NOTES

4. Adam Smith, op. cit., Book I, Ch. 2, p. 119.
5. Michael Oakeshott, *Rationalism in Politics and other Essays*, Methuen, 1962, p. 4.
6. Quoted by Ralph Harris, *Morality and Markets*, Centre for Policy Studies, 1986, p. 2.
7. Ibid., p. 2.
8. Ibid., pp. 2–3.
9. Joseph Schumpeter, op. cit., p. 143.

CHAPTER VII

1. Viscount Hailsham, *The Conservative Case*, Penguin, 1959, p. 57.
2. See also Daniel Bell, *The Cultural Contradictions of Capitalism*, Basic Books, 1978, and Fred Hirsch, *The Social Limits to Growth*, Routledge & Kegan Paul, 1977.
3. Daniel Bell, op. cit., p. 71.
4. David Hume, 'Of Refinement in the Arts', in *Essays, Moral and Political*, Oxford, 1963, pp. 277–8. See also Hume's essays: 'Of Civil Liberty', 'Of the Rise and Progress of the Arts and Sciences', 'Of Commerce'.
5. Walter Bagehot, *The English Constitution*, Fontana, 1963, p. 236.
6. Edmund Burke, *Reflections on the Revolution in France*, Penguin, 1986, p. 183.
7. Adam Smith, *Wealth of Nations*, Penguin, 1986, Book III, Ch. 4, p. 508.
8. Robert Axelrod, *The Evolution of Co-operation*, Penguin, 1990.
9. Beatrice Webb, *My Apprenticeship*, Penguin, 1971, p. 166.
10. Ibid., p. 175.
11. Ibid., p. 178.
12. Quoted in Robert Colls and Phillip Dodd (eds), *Englishness, Politics and Culture 1880–1920*, Croom Helm, 1986, p. 1.
13. See ibid., a fascinating collection of essays.
14. For a discussion of this question of 'evolutionary conservatism' see John Gray, *Hayek on Liberty*, Blackwell, 1984, p. 41ff.

CHAPTER VIII

1. R. H. Tawney, *Equality*, 1931, quoted in Keith Joseph and Jonathan Sumption, *Equality*, Murray, 1979, p. 11.
2. Edmund Burke, *Reflections on the Revolution in France*, Penguin, 1986, p. 150.
3. John Rawls, *Theory of Justice*, OUP, 1971, p. 303.
4. This point is made in Isaiah Berlin, 'Equality', *Proceedings of the Aristotelian Society 1955–56*, pp. 301–26.
5. Alexis de Tocqueville, *Democracy in America*, OUP, 1946, pp. 3, 9.

CHAPTER IX

1. 'Mumbo-jumbo' is the term which Peter Jenkins, for example, uses in his book *Mrs Thatcher's Revolution*, Cape, 1987.
2. David Hume, 'Of Money' in *Essays, Moral and Political*, OUP, 1963, pp. 293–4.
3. New York *Times*, 22 July 1990.

CHAPTER X

1. Leslie Hannah traces the emergence of the compulsory retirement age to the 1890s: see *Inventing Retirement: The Development of Occupational Pensions in Britain*, CUP, 1986, pp. 134–6.
2. A speech made by Winston Churchill on 2 March 1944, quoted in Martin Gilbert, *Churchill*, Vol. III: *Road to Victory: 1941–45*, Heinemann, 1986, p. 651.
3. F. A. Hayek, *Constitution of Liberty*, Routledge & Kegan Paul, 1960, pp. 257–8.
4. Ibid., p. 289.

CHAPTER XI

1. Edmund Burke, 'Letter to a Noble Lord', quoted in Stanley Ayling, *Edmund Burke*, Cassell, 1988, p. 267.

2. Walter Bagehot, *The English Constitution*, Fontana, 1963, pp. 265–6.

3. David Ogg, *England in the Reign of James II and William III*, OUP, 1969, pp. 241–2.

4. Douglas Hurd, R. A. Butler Memorial Lecture, 10 February 1989.

5 Ibid.

6. See, for example, John Patten's pamphlet *Political Culture, Conservatism, and Rolling Constitutional Change*, Conservative Political Centre, 1991.

7. Quoted by Alistair Cooke in *Proportional Representation*, Conservative Research Department Paper No. 15, 1983, p. 277.

8. Ibid., p. 275.

9. Quoted in Sir Angus Maude and John Szemerey, *Why Electoral Change?*, Conservative Political Centre, 1982, p. 30.

10. Alistair Cooke, op. cit., p. 276.

11. Michael Oakeshott, *Rationalism in Politics and other Essays*, Methuen, 1962, p. 40.

CHAPTER XII

1. As William Wallace points out in *The Transformation of Western Europe*, Royal Institute of International Affairs, 1990.

2. Sir Geoffrey Howe, 'Sovereignty and Interdependence: Britain's Place in the World', *International Affairs*, Vol. 66, No. 4, 1990, p. 675.

3. Quoted by Hugh Conningham, 'The Conservative Party and Patriotism' in Robert Colls and Phillip Dodd (eds), *Englishness, Politics and Culture 1880–1920*, Croom Helm, 1986, p. 301.

4. The best account of the significance of the internal market is to be found in Nicholas Colchester and David Buchan, *Europe Relaunched: Truth and Illusions on the Way to 1992*, Economist Books, 1990.

5. See the discussion in Andrew Tyrie, *A Cautionary Tale of EMU*, Centre for Policy Studies, 1991.

CONCLUSION

1. Edmund Burke, *Thoughts and Details on Scarcity*, quoted in Ian Hampsher-Monk, *Philosophy of Edmund Burke*, Longman, 1987, pp. 278–9.
2. Edmund Burke, *Reflections on the Revolution in France*, Penguin, 1986, pp. 239–40.

INDEX